The Guiding Star families need for autism, ADD/ADHD, psychiatric, developmental, or special health needs

Family Road Map

A Step-By-Step Guide to Navigating Health, Education, and Insurance Services for Families with Special Needs

By Wendy Lowe Besmann

with **Kimberly Douglass**, PhD, **Keva Clark**, M.Ed, **Angela Lassiter**, CPSP *and*
Kathy Bentley, M.A., **Wanda Cummings**, MSW, CPSS
Maryann Donovan, CPSP, **Susan Emley**, **Heather Hall**,
Crystal Karenchak, **Wendy Pennington**, M.A.
and **Susan Wood**

TEAM UP *for* **FAMILIES**
COLABORACIÓN *para* **FAMILIAS**

Melton Hill Media
9119 Solway Ferry Road
Oak Ridge, Tennessee
37830
www.meltonhillmedia.com

Several training curricula in English and Spanish have been developed for use of this book with parents, family advocates, and case managers by Team Up for Families (TUFF), an educational initiative of Melton Hill Media, LLC, and Family Road Map Institute, a training academy and learning portal. For information, please contact wendy@teamupforfamilies.org.

Printed in the United States of America. This book is printed on acid-free paper.
Last digit is print number: 9 8 7 6 5 4 3 2 1

Published by Melton Hill Media, LLC. 9119 Solway Ferry Road
Oak Ridge, TN 37830 www.meltonhillmedia.com

Library of Congress Cataloging-in-Publication Data
Besmann, Wendy Lowe
Family Road Map: *A Step-by-Step Guide to Navigating Health, Education, and Insurance Services for Families with Special Needs.*

Includes bibliographical references
ISBN-13 978-0-9816793-3-4
1. Special Education (General)
2. Special Education (Intellectual and Developmental)
3. Special Education (Behavioral and Emotional)

Table of Contents

About the Author

Wendy Lowe Besmann is the director of Team Up for Families, a na-tional learning collaborative dedicated to helping families get better services. A longtime writer and behavioral health advocate, she is the mother of a son with autism and bipolar disorder. Besmann has contributed articles to national publications that include *Better Homes and Gardens*, *USA Today*, *Emotional and Behavioral Disorders in Youth*, *The New York Times*, and *Parenting*.

A native Californian, she has lived for many years in Tennessee, where she served in leadership positions with her local and state NAMI (National Alliance on Mental Illness) affiliates and mental health/developmental disability policy councils. She also trained staff in High-Fidelity Wraparound for K-Town Youth Empowerment Network, a system of care for transition-age youth in Knox County, Tennessee.

Team Up for Families (TUFF) and Family Road Map Institute

This guide is adapted from *Team Up for Your Child* (2008, 2012) and *Road Map workshops* (2014-2016), created by Melton Hill Media, LLC, through its Team Up for Families initiative. TUFF Certified Trainers from Maine to Hawaii brought this guide and curriculum to nearly 500 family members in their own communities. In 2017, TUFF leaders created the Family Road Map Institute, a training academy and learning portal dedicated to providing information and resources to families and agencies that serve children, youth, and young adults.

2017 Family Road Map Editorial Team

TUFF Collaborative members reviewed and provided editing assistance to transform the original *Team Up for Your Child* 2nd Edition text into *Family Road Map*: Kimberly Douglass, Associate Professor of the School of Information Sciences, University of Tennessee, Knoxville; Angela Lassiter, TUFF Administrative Lead; and Keva Clark, National Collaborative Lead; TUFF Master Trainers Kathy Bentley, Wanda Cummings, Susan Emley, Crystal Karenchak, and Susan Wood; TUFF/Melton Hill Media Strategic Lead Heather Hall, and TUFF Certified Trainers Maryann Donovan and Wendy Pennington.

Pilot Advisory Committee and Sponsors

This book was originally developed in 2006-2007 as *Team Up for Your Child*, a pilot project sponsored by NAMI (National Alliance for Mental Illness) Tennessee. The 23 health and education specialists listed below reviewed the material numerous times, offering invaluable suggestions and critique. The author is especially grateful to Sita Diehl, former Director of Policy and State Outreach, Advocacy and Public Policy, NAMI, and Roger Stewart, Deputy Director of NAMI Tennessee, for believing in this project from the beginning. Sixteen Tennessee state and local organizations and other funding sources provided support for the project.

Pilot Advisory Edition Sponsors: We gratefully acknowledge financial support for the 2007 pilot edition from the following: Cherokee Health Systems, Child and Family Tennessee, East Tennessee Children's Hospital, Family Practice Associates, Helen Ross McNabb Center, Katharine Collins Roddy and J.P. Roddy, Sr. Fund of East Tennessee Foundation, Knox County Schools, Janssen Pharmaceutica, Magellan Health Services Tennessee Care Management Center, Mental Illness Awareness Coalition, NAMI Knoxville, Parent-Child Services Group, Inc., Peninsula, Project GRAD Knoxville, Ridgeview Resources for Living, and Tennessee Voices for Children.

Pilot Edition Advisory Committee: William Allen, *PhD*; William Berez, *PhD*; Brian Bonfardin, *MD*; Drema Bowers, *MSSW*; Donna Flanery; Bobby Brown, *MSSW, LCSW*; Charlotte Bryson, *MA*; Karen Loy, *EdD*; Melissa Massie, *MS*; Carletta Rando-Smelcer, *MA*; Ronda Redden Reitz, *PhD*; Archie Carden, *EdD*; Monica Causey, *CMSW*; Sita Diehl, *MA, MSSW*; Joshua Gettinger, *MD*; Jim Griffin, *MSSW, LCSW*; Lynne F. Harmon, *MA, CCC-SLP*; Barbara Levin, *MD, MPH*; Debby Lovin-Buuck, *MSSW, LCSW*; Karen Sowers, *PhD*; Mike Sterling, *MSSW, LCSW*; Nicole Swain, *PsyD*; Anne Burnett Young, *MS, CAS*.

Credits

Design and production by Veronika Grebbenikova; Interior Illustration and cover design by Barbara Boeing, Boeing Design & Illustration, bboeing@comcast.net.

Copy-editing by Heather Hall and Em Turner Chitty, Em Turner English Services, etchitty@gmail.com.

Welcome to the Road Map

Empowering the Journey to Help and Hope

When a child has serious problems, parents enter a strange new world. In this new world, most of the ordinary rules for raising kids don't seem to work. Something's wrong, but very often you don't know why or what to do. Friends and family give all sorts of opinions. It can seem like the tension around your house never quits. Who knows what's best? Who has the answers? How will you pay for this? Maybe you feel stressed out, angry, or just plain confused. Breaking down that confusion into manageable parts is what this book is all about.

If you are the parent of a young person with special needs, you tend to lose a lot of sleep. You worry about what will happen in the future. You worry about all the simple, fun things your child is missing. As time goes on, you may start to feel cut off from that other world of "normal" families whose lives have typical routines and whose kids seem to act in ways that other people understand.

You worry most of all about finding the right help, and that often means dealing with a lot of different providers. **Providers** is the term used in this book for the people and agencies who provide services for your child. Sometimes their language is filled with long, unfamiliar words. People with clipboards ask a lot of personal questions. You read forms, fill out forms, and sign more forms. It can feel overwhelming.

Team David: Our Road to a "New Reality"

At age three, our son David was diagnosed with autism. By age five, he was also diagnosed with bipolar disorder. For quite a few years, life in our house was tough. David would wake up from every nap screaming uncontrollably. Day after day, we coped with a child who suddenly exploded in a fit of scratching and biting. He didn't sleep through the night until he was five, and wasn't toilet-trained until age seven. He couldn't hold a real conversation until many years later. He spent a week in a psychiatric hospital. When my cell phone rang on a school day, it usually meant bad news. As he got bigger, life got scarier--and of course, we grieved for the "normal" life we couldn't have.

Little by little, something changed. We learned to reach out for help. With good treatment and the right support system, our son's functioning improved beyond anything we could have imagined. Today--in his 20s-- David lives independently in his own housing and takes care of everyday needs such as riding the bus, shopping, and cooking. He likes stocking shelves at a local store. He is passionate about collecting dinosaur figures, making short videos, and visiting natural history museums. We have a network of friends and helpers we call "Team David" who drop by on a regular basis. There are challenges, but all in all, things are good.

Through the years, our family learned ways to find support. Our job was to build a "new reality" that made sense for the life we live. To do it, we had to work as full, equal team partners with David's providers.

For All Kinds of Parents, Children, and Youth

The term "parent" in this book is meant to include grandparents, other relatives, legal guardians, adoptive parents, and foster parents who face the challenges of raising children or youth with medical, developmental, behavioral, and other complex health needs or learning differences. In some parts of this book, the term "child" is used, while in other parts, the term "child or youth" is used. This serves as a reminder that many of the strategies in this book apply to every age and stage of a young person's journey to wellness.

Welcome to the Road Map

Different Ways to Say It

Different organizations may use different terms. A health issue of any type may affect a child's development or behavior, and those problems may affect physical health. Sometimes behavioral health is called "mental health" and a behavioral health issue may be called a "mental illness."

A behavioral health issue that seriously disrupts a child's life may be called a "Serious Emotional Disturbance (SED)," particularly in educational systems. Attention Deficit Hyperactivity Disorder (ADHD) and other developmental disorders, such as autism, can also create behavioral health and physical health problems that need treatment.

Bottom line: Whatever labels are used by providers and insurers, it is vital to treat the whole child!

Who's on Your Team?

"Special needs" is a way of describing a child's or youth's problems with functioning or managing everyday activities. For most, it's rarely just one need! "Special health needs" is a term that includes the needs of children with various medical issues and one or more physical, behavioral, or developmental problems. "Behavioral health" generally describes a person's ability to act and to cope with emotions. "Developmental" issues or disorders refer to a child's/youth's functioning in everyday life compared to others of his or her age. "Learning" or "sensory" disorders can relate to developmental issues early in life.

Most special needs services involve more than one system. Your child's team may include many members, such as doctors and therapists, health workers, or a case manager. It may also include government agencies, the school system, or an insurance program. You might deal with some people a few times and others for many years.

Family-Tested Strategies

No matter what titles these providers wear, you are the "facilitator" of this team. Our health and educational systems can be so disconnected that the other members need YOU to make sure they work together. Each provider helps with different parts of your child's situation, but quite often, people in different systems can't or won't talk to each other. YOU are the only one who takes care of the whole child. That doesn't mean you need to run everything or know everything. You can't be an expert on every part of your child's treatment or education. Your job is to empower yourself to keep the team moving in the right direction. It can be simpler than you may think!

Family Road Map is a step-by-step guide to working with your child's team. This book is full of real ideas used by real families who face many of the same challenges you face. I call these "family-tested strategies." Some of these ideas were shared by our Team Up for Families (TUFF)/Family Road Map Certified Trainers and Facilitators, who lead workshops and support groups in their own communities based on the material in this book. You can find out more about this network at http://teamupforfamilies.org. Other strategies were suggested by people who work and volunteer in advocacy organizations such as National Federation of Families for Children's Mental Health, NAMI (National Alliance on Mental Illness), developmental disabilities councils, and other health advocacy organizations.

Living with a child who has special needs is rarely easy. Every day, we're all just trying to figure it out. *Family Road Map* can help you break down what may at, times, seem like a big awful mess into small tasks you can handle. Remember: You CAN do it—and only you can do it!

Take care and good luck!

Wendy Lowe Besmann
wendy@teamupforfamilies.org

The Five-Point Guiding Star to Navigating Systems

The process of finding your way through all the complicated procedures and paperwork to get services for your child is called "navigating a system." Over the years, most families travel through many systems with very different rules, providers, and procedures. Plus, systems themselves keep changing as new programs come and go. How do you navigate through a confusing world where the landmarks keep shifting? The answer is to use your *Guiding Star*.

The five points on the *Guiding Star* are five tasks that will keep you oriented and on the right road--no matter what system you are navigating. The *Guiding Star* can help you sort through the confusion and chunk up a big job into tasks you can handle. It can also help you get respect from the providers on your team, and better results in any system.

This book is organized around step-by-step ways to navigate a system, using all five points of the *Guiding Star**.

1 **Set GOALS**
Decide what you are looking for based on the strengths and concerns of your child or youth, and your family (including yourself). Life is simpler when everyone on your team understands your child's or youth's--and your family's--priorities.

5 **Find SUPPORT**
Find people and resources to help you cope with challenges and create the future you want for your family.

2 **Learn SYSTEM BASICS**
Become familiar with key words, procedures, and provider roles so you understand what choices you have, where to find services, and how to get those services.

4 **Manage INFORMATION**
Keep good records. Observe and report on your child's or youth's progress. Insist on clear explanations for any data (such as test scores) that are used to make decisions about treatment or services.

3 **Build RELATIONSHIPS**
Communicate clearly, and show you expect to be included in all decisions as a full partner. Find people who can help you meet goals, handle system barriers, and solve problems.

*(Special thanks to Team Up for Families/Family Road Map Learning Collaborative Administrator and Certified Trainer Angela Lassiter, who named this five-point process our "**Guiding Star**.")*

Welcome to the Road Map

Those L-o-o-n-g, Confusing Words

Medical, behavioral health, education, and insurance providers use a lot of technical language. For plain definitions of words printed like **this** *in the pages of Family Road Map, see the Glossary, page 91.*

Symbols in This Book

 Keywords and definitions of common terms you may encounter in dealing with providers, schools, insurance companies, and others

 Family-tested strategies

 Materials available in Spanish

 Useful print resource

 Important alerts

 Lists or sample forms to fill in

 Tips for taming paperwork

 Try this

 Useful online (website) resource

 Tales from Team David

Guiding Star Point One: Set GOALS

Choosing a Path

Sometimes you may know exactly what you're looking for when you begin to navigate a system. More often, it's complicated. Before you hit the road, it can be vital to figure out what types of fuel and provisions you already have on board. That's why the first point of the Guiding Star (which is rooted in family-driven, person-centered care) begins with the strengths of your child or youth and family. An empowered parent takes note of anything positive that might be put to good use by some creative thinker on your team. Once you start identifying strengths, the most amazing things can happen. Don't forget to think about your own strengths—you'll need them!

The next step is to look at some of the concerns you have about your child or youth. It helps many parents to think in terms of concerns that are short-term ("What will happen at school next month?") and longer-term ("What will happen when she grows up?"), so you and your team can begin to set priorities.

Strengths, Concerns & "The Big Picture"

You can use the worksheets on the next three pages to start the conversation. Filling them out can help you think about and list some general areas you want to discuss with health and education providers. The first sheet is for your child or youth. The next two sheets are for you.

Strengths: What does your child or youth like doing or take pride in doing? What skills does he or she have that are useful in everyday life? What qualities does this child have that could "shine through" more brightly when other problems are handled? What strengths do you have as a parent? What strengths in your family, friends, and other close relationships might support you on this journey?

Concerns: Think about these areas as they relate to your child:
- Physical and emotional health
- Relationships with friends, family, teachers, neighbors
- Changes in behavior or school performance
- Communication (ability to express thoughts/understand others)
- Mobility (ease in getting around independently)
- Changes in the family situation (such as divorce or difficult events)

Picturing the Best Your Child or Youth Can Be

The final step in this Guiding Star Point is to begin looking at "The Big Picture." This is a vision for the very best your child or youth can be. Different members of the team—including your child or youth—may have very different ideas about "The Big Picture." Filling out the worksheet on page 10 can help you think about "The Big Picture."

Hope Makes Things Happen

The right treatment can make amazing changes in your child's life. Try picturing that life—your family's life—as if it were scenes from a movie you would all like to watch. What would that movie look like?

You aren't just daydreaming. Looking at "The Big Picture" means trying to define what your child can do and be. It means helping your older child or youth begin to imagine a better life. Some of these hopes will help the team set long-term goals. "The Big Picture" can make a really big difference.

SET GOALS

Speaking Up

On this sheet, write down some things you want people to know about you. Everybody has things they like about themselves and their lives. Everybody has things they wish they could change. People in your life may already be asking you some of these questions. It's good to think about them on your own time, so you can say what you really mean. Your feelings and needs matter! Knowing what you want will make it easier to get the help you need.

*Ask for this page to be copied if you want to fill it out privately. This is your choice.

My name is:_____

Some things I like to do are:_____
_____
_____
_____
_____

Things I like best about myself:_____
_____
_____
_____

Things I worry about sometimes:_____
_____
_____
_____

Things I do sometimes, but I don't know why:
_____
_____
_____
_____

If I could change something about my life or myself, it would be:_____
_____
_____
_____

What really makes me feel good is:_____
_____
_____
_____

In the future, I hope I can:_____
_____
_____
_____

My Child's/Youth's & Family's Strengths and Concerns

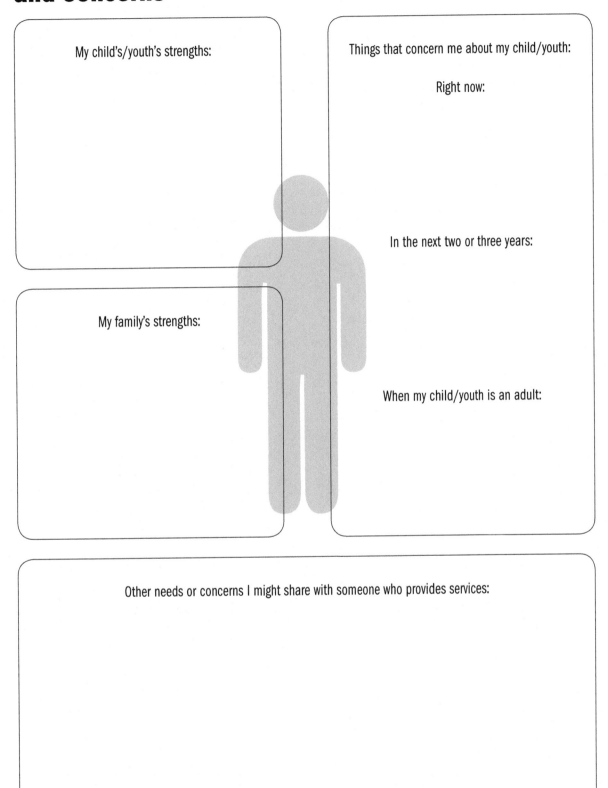

My child's/youth's strengths:

Things that concern me about my child/youth:

Right now:

In the next two or three years:

My family's strengths:

When my child/youth is an adult:

Other needs or concerns I might share with someone who provides services:

How I Picture the Best My Child/Youth Can Be

My child's/youth's daily behavior at home would look like:

My child's/youth's social life and friendships would look like:

My child's/youth's free time activities would look like:

Success for my child/youth at school would be:

Our family life would look like:

Other hopes, plans and dreams for my child's/youth's future:

Other things I want people who work with us to know about my child/youth and family:

Guiding Star Point Two: Learn SYSTEM BASICS

Key Words for First Steps

Most parents begin with a pressing need to know, "What's wrong with our child? What do we CALL it?" We all tend to feel as if putting a label on this strange behavior will give us some power to find the magic cure. The trouble is that a child's or youth's behavior is never a perfect match with any label.

A **diagnosis** is the overall term that health providers use to describe a problem. It is reached by gathering enough evidence (facts) to make an evaluation (conclusions about what's going on and what to do about it). **Evidence** may come from conversations with you, your child, and others. Other facts may come from a physical examination, tests, or laboratory studies. The **evaluation** and diagnosis may be used to make a **treatment plan** (steps each member of the team will do to work on the problem) or inform others. These facts may also be used to decide whether your child can get certain mental health expenses paid for by your insurance plan. These facts may also help determine whether your child can receive special services at school.

A diagnosis is a guideline, not a recipe! Children's bodies, brains, and emotions are different. Those differences will affect the kinds of medications or therapies that work best. Sometimes, a child meets some of the **criteria** (types of behavior) for another disorder, which will be called a **secondary** or **comorbid diagnosis**. The diagnosis may change as your child grows or as more information is gathered.

Where to Start

The first step is to have the child examined by a **primary care provider**. This person is sometimes known as a "**primary care practitioner**," or "**family medicine practitioner**." The primary care provider may be a **pediatrician** (a medical doctor specializing in children's overall healthcare). In some cases, you will see a **Nurse Practitioner** (**NP**). Even if the doctor has already done a regular physical exam, he or she may order special tests or ask different questions. Some behavioral problems can be caused by physical conditions; for example, certain brain injuries or fevers may affect behavior. Also, some health problems may lead to behavioral or emotional issues. If that's the case, your doctor may want to refer you to a medical specialist or a behavioral health specialist. If your child doesn't seem to be developing certain types of skills in the same way as most children of the same age, the doctor may also refer you to a developmental health specialist. Some of these specialties are described on the next page.

Be sure to bring this physical examination record to any specialists who evaluate or treat your child, since they may not do full examinations themselves. This information is also important when you fill out **health history forms**, which you may need to do each time you visit a new provider.

Know Your Support Staff

Receptionists, physicians' assistants, administrators, technicians, and nurses can be great sources of information about how things work in a provider's office or clinic. Take time to notice them, learn their names, and ask for their advice.

Ask Again!

If you don't understand an explanation the first time, try asking the question a different way. For example, you might say "Can you run that by me again, please?" or "Could you break that down for me? I didn't quite get all of it." That way, neither of you is embarrassed--but the provider realizes you intend to get a clear answer before you make any decisions. Most providers will respect that!

In some rural counties and other areas that are short on behavioral health providers, the pediatrician or other primary care doctor may prescribe medications for behavioral health issues. (Some primary care doctors and pediatricians have special training in behavioral health issues.) In some cases, a doctor may order a blood test or other procedure (such as an MRI) to find out if a medical condition is causing your child's atypical behavior.

However, it is important to know that no current medical test can diagnose conditions such as ADHD or anxiety. The provider has to rely on observation and information provided by you, others, and your child or youth.

NOTE: If your child begins treatment with a psychiatrist or other behavioral health specialist, be sure to keep the primary care provider informed and involved. For example, certain medications for ADHD or **mood disorders** can affect a child's weight or risk for diseases such as diabetes. If so, your primary care doctor can work with you on a plan to prevent or treat such conditions before they become big problems for your child.

Discuss the matter with your child's or youth's classroom teacher or school counselor, as well. They may notice many behaviors you may not see at home. They can also give you a better idea of how your child is acting or developing compared to other children of that age.

IF YOU ARE CONFUSED ABOUT ANYTHING, ASK TO HAVE THE PROCESS EXPLAINED TO YOU. It is always better to get the ALL the information you need to make the best decisions for your child or youth.

The best way to get the information you need is to ask questions that begin with **Who...? What...? When...? Where...? Why....? How...?** and **Can you explain...?**

For example, you might ask:

Who will we need to see next?

What will happen next?

Where will this happen?

When can we expect this to happen?

How can I contact you or that person?

Why is my child seeing this specialist?

Can you explain how this process works?

Medical, behavioral, and developmental health specialists who may evaluate your child/youth include:

MEDICAL DOCTORS AND NURSES who can prescribe medications:

Psychiatrist: A medical doctor who is trained to evaluate and treat your child's or youth's behavior, primarily by prescribing medications. A psychiatrist has the most formal training in behavioral health, but may spend the least amount of time with you and your child during treatment

Behavioral/Developmental Pediatrician: Combines physical, psychological, and developmental evaluations, as well as treatment.

Neurologist: Medical doctor who specializes in how the brain functions physically and chemically.

Licensed Psychiatric Nurse Practitioner: Assists in or performs clinical evaluations, designs treatment plans, and may provide counseling, medication management, and/or other treatment.

BEHAVIORAL (MENTAL) HEALTH PROVIDERS who may evaluate or treat, but do NOT prescribe medications:

Clinical Psychologist: Licensed by the state to evaluate your child's behavioral health and academic performance. May also provide psychotherapy, a form of counseling that is commonly known as "talk therapy," but may include other kinds of one-on-one or group treatment.

School Psychologist: Employed by the school system to do various evaluations. May provide a "psycho-educational" evaluation to determine your child's or youth's skills and ability to learn compared to other children and youth of the same age. A psycho-educational evaluation does not diagnose mental illness. However, it may be used to determine a child's or youth's need for special school services.

Licensed Clinical Social Worker: Licensed by the state to provide one-on-one or group therapy.

Counseling and Evaluation Providers: Some providers (including those listed above) may have other titles, such as Licensed Psychological Examiner, Licensed Marriage and Family Therapist, Licensed Professional Counselor, or Licensed Substance Abuse Counselor. Feel free to ask questions about the therapist's training. His or her license should be posted somewhere in the building.

Straight Talk

Sometimes it can be very hard to speak frankly about a child's or youth's problems. You may wonder if you are "making too much of it." It may not be part of your culture to tell personal information to people outside the family. Parents or others in the family may strongly disagree with one another about what is really happening. In any case, it is very important to state the facts as clearly and plainly as you can from your own point of view. Tell the provider exactly what you observed, what you think, and what you feel. You are the expert on your child or youth. You are helping him or her understand the importance of speaking plainly and honestly with a provider. See "Getting Ready for Intake Interviews" on page 15 for more ideas.

Who's Who in Mental Health Counseling

Few sources are better than the website Mental Health America, run by the Mental Health Association. It offers a huge amount of practical information about mental health disorders and treatment. It's a good place to look for information about local services and support. You can also find good definitions of mental health counseling specialties. www.mentalhealthamerica. net/types-mental-health-professionals.

DEVELOPMENTAL SPECIALISTS <u>who may evaluate or treat your child/youth</u>:

Speech Language Pathologist (**SLP**): Evaluates and treats the way a child understands and uses communication. This includes spoken language plus "non-verbal" signals, such as eye contact and body language. The SLP deals with how sounds are pronounced ("articulation") and voice quality ("hoarseness, pitch"). The SLP also studies "social language" (ability to understand social cues, talk back and forth with someone or solve problems through communication). The SLP may do therapy for oral skills, such as feeding (in some places this is done by an occupational therapist), or academic skills, such as reading. The SLP may also develop picture/symbol systems that help a non-verbal person to communicate.

Occupational Therapist: Evaluates and treats problems with fine motor skills (use of the small muscles of the body, such as those in arms and hands), daily living skills (such as eating or dressing), visual-perceptual skills, motor skills (such as writing), or pre-vocational skills (such as following a set of instructions). An OT may evaluate and treat "sensory integration" problems (how a person's brain understands and responds to signals from the five senses).

Physical Therapist: Evaluates and treats problems with gross motor skills (use of large muscles of the body such as those in arms and legs), strength, movement, and mobility. The PT may use massage, movement, and special equipment, such as a walker or wheelchair, to help a person move around more independently.

Audiologist: Evaluates the way sounds are heard or understood by the brain. This person may evaluate how loud a sound needs to be for a person to hear it, or whether the brain "reads" that sound correctly.

Behavior Analyst: Provides evaluation of behavioral problems to determine why they occur. Develops a plan to change the behavior or environment. This specialist sometimes uses a method called Applied Behavioral Analysis (ABA).

Special Education Teacher: A teacher who is specially licensed to work with a wide range of students who may have physical, behavioral, intellectual, developmental, emotional, physical, or learning disabilities.

Getting Ready for Intake Interviews

An **intake interview** is the first appointment with a new health provider or agency. At this appointment, you will be asked to tell the provider about your child or youth and discuss his or her symptoms. **Symptoms** are signs of **disorders** (physical changes, thoughts, feelings, or behaviors that cause problems with functioning in everyday life.)

Learning how to sum up your concerns clearly is important for many reasons. First, the appointment time goes by very quickly, so you want to make the most of the time you have. Second, the behavior your child shows during an office visit may be very different from the way he or she acts at home. It will help the provider if you can describe typical home behavior. Third, you will probably have to fill out a questionnaire that includes this same information. (Sometimes the provider will ask questions from a list and write down the answers.) Doing this will help you gather your thoughts ahead of time. Fourth, you can let the provider know which concerns you (and your child/youth) think are most important. That helps you act as equal partners in making treatment decisions.

Most parents end up repeating this same "strengths and concerns story" to different providers on the team. The method described below can help boil it down to the basics.

Five Steps to Describing a "Strengths and Concerns Story"

On the next few pages, you will find a five-step process to help you describe medical, behavioral, and developmental concerns during an intake interview. The health provider needs to know about all three areas because everything in your child's body is connected. For example, certain behavior symptoms can be signs of thyroid disease, a medical condition. Certain physical ailments, such as frequent headaches and stomachaches, can be symptoms of a mood disorder. A child who gets very upset or irritable in noisy places may have a developmental problem (such as a sensory disorder). In each case, finding the root cause or causes will help the child get better treatment.

- *Step One: Consider Medical (Physical) Concerns*

- *Step Two: Consider Behavioral Concerns*

- *Step Three: Consider Developmental Concerns*

- *Step Four: Identify Top Three Concerns*

- *Step Five: Sum Up Strengths and Concerns*

FAQs

The National Institute for Mental Health offers a useful booklet on what to do if you suspect your child has a behavioral health issue. Go to www.nimh.nih.gov/health/publications/index.shtml. The homepage includes a summary of the most common childhood mental disorders. It describes the treatments and medications most often used, and it answers frequently asked questions. You can order free booklets in English or Spanish.

Step One: Consider Medical (Physical) Concerns

Check the conditions that have occurred "Never, Occasionally, Often, or Very Often" in the last six months.

	Never	Occasionally	Often	Very Often
1. Headaches				
2. Stomachaches				
3. Fever				
4. Dizziness				
5. Tires easily				
6. Sleeps much more than usual				
7. Sleeps less or complains of being unable to sleep				
8. Low energy				
9. Unexplained rashes				
10. Recent weight gain				
11. Recent weight loss				
12. Vision problems				
13. Hearing problems				
14. Ear infections				
Other Ailments:				

SUICIDE AND VIOLENCE RISK

If your child shows any of these signs:
Sudden change in personality
Gives away many favorite possessions
Talks of wanting to die or "disappear"
Takes unusual risks or shows reckless behavior
Threatens suicide or violence
Talks of family or others being "better off without me"
Has a sudden and frequent interest in death or methods of dying
Collects objects that may cause harm to self or others
TAKE IT SERIOUSLY. DO NOT DELAY. Seek immediate help from your doctor. In a crisis situation, call your local Specialized Crisis Services phone number. If you can't find this number, call the nearest psychiatric hospital for information or call 911. Staff will come help you determine if your child needs emergency care.
See Guiding Star Point 5 for more on "Family Crisis Survival Guide."

Step Two: Consider Behavioral Concerns

Rate concerns as occurring "Never, Occasionally, Often, or Very Often" in the last six months. At the bottom of page 18, add any other concerns not on this list.

	Never	Occasionally	Often	Very Often
1. Often loses personal items (ex. clothes, textbooks).				
2. Doesn't pay attention to details on homework.				
3. Has trouble paying attention to jobs or chores at home.				
4. Has trouble getting organized to do schoolwork.				
5. Doesn't play with other children.				
6. Pulls out hair from head or body.				
7. Lines up objects rather than playing with them.				
8. Lectures children on a high-interest topic, even when they seem uninterested.				
9. Has trouble sharing with other children.				
10. Has trouble playing quiet activities.				
11. Has trouble changing from one activity to another.				
12. Gets overexcited or overstressed, even at fun occasions (e.g. birthday parties).				
13. Grades have dropped a lot recently.				
14. Teachers report more "acting out" behavior.				
15. Teachers report child seems more "sad" or "lost" lately.				
16. Has tantrums or shows unusually angry behavior when other children win at games.				
17. Becomes giddy or irritable for no apparent reason; a short time later is quiet and sad.				
18. Eats very little in order to lose weight, even though already thin.				
19. Recently shows little interest in spending time with friends.				
20. Fights with other children.				
21. Starts many projects without finishing them.				
22. Can't seem to sit still even when trying to do so.				
23. Is fearful of going to school.				
24. Is easily frustrated.				
25. Has temper tantrums.				
26. Gets very anxious or worries a lot.				
27. Has fixed "rituals" that he/she needs to do to in order feel okay.				
28. Destroys objects.				
29. Has deliberately set fires.				
30. Has hurt others on purpose.				
31. Deliberately destroys property of others.				
32. Has used a weapon that can cause serious harm.				
33. Has run away from home overnight.				
34. Has stayed out at night without permission.				
35. Says he/she feels worthless or inferior.				

Behavioral Concerns, continued

	Never	Occasionally	Often	Very Often
36. Says, "No one loves me."				
37. Has committed a crime.				
38. Feels guilty, thinks problems are "all my fault."				
39. Seems sad, lonely, or depressed.				
40. Is cruel to animals.				
41. Is physically cruel to others.				
42. Has trouble making friends.				
43. Has trouble keeping friends.				
44. Gets embarrassed very easily.				
45. Seems unusually shy with others.				
46. Is afraid to try new things due to fear of making a mistake.				
47. Lies to or "cons" others to get out of trouble, avoid things, or get things.				
48. Fidgets with hands or feet.				
49. Leaves seat at school or elsewhere when supposed to stay seated.				
50. Has difficulty waiting his or her turn.				
51. Interrupts others' conversations.				
52. Bullies or threatens others.				
53. Is angry and resentful.				
54. Acts on impulse.				
55. Defies adults or refuses to go along with requests and rules, despite possibility of punishment.				
56. Talks too much or too rapidly.				
57. Is easily annoyed by others.				
58. Blames others for his/her mistakes or behavior.				
59. Doesn't seem to listen when spoken to directly.				
60. Doesn't like to be touched.				
61. Skips school without permission.				
62. Has stolen valuable things.				
63. Argues with those in authority.				
Other symptoms:				

Sources: American Academy of Pediatrics, North Carolina Center for Children's Healthcare Improvement, National Initiative for Children's Healthcare Quality, NICHQ Vanderbilt Assessment Scale-Parent Informant. In: Caring for Children with ADHD: A Resource Toolkit for Clinicians. Elk Grove Village, IL; American Academy of Pediatrics; 2005. Additional source: "Pediatric Symptom Checklist" by Michael Jellinek, MD, and Michael Murphy, EdD, Massachusetts General Hospital, Boston, MA. Additional material from ADHD Checklist by Linda Zweifel, Director of Programs, NAMI Montgomery County, Texas; adapted with permission from author.

Step Three: Consider Developmental Concerns

Children develop at different speeds, but most gain certain skills at roughly the same ages. You don't have to be an expert to notice that your child seems to be developing more slowly or has very different behaviors from other children in the same age group. Developmental differences don't necessarily mean your child has, or will have, a disability. They may simply be signs that your child needs some form of short-term therapy. On the other hand, if a disorder such as autism is present, it is extremely important to diagnose and start services as soon as possible. In any case, if you feel uneasy about the way your child is developing, check it out. Here are some categories to consider (**Remember: These skills are compared with other children of the same age.** For example, few three-year-olds zip their own coats, but most six-year-olds can.)

Sensory Processing: How does the child learn best—by seeing, hearing, smelling, tasting, or touching? How does this affect daily life?_____

_____

Sensory Modulation: Does he/she seem to react too much or not enough to sounds, touch, or light? Do rough clothes, new shoes, or shirt tags make him/her unable to concentrate? Does he/she avoid certain "normal" sensations or seek them out?_____

_____

Communication: When did your child begin to babble? Speak in words? String words into simple sentences? Does your child (above age 2) use back-and-forth talk with others? Use conversation to ask for things and information?_____

_____

_____

Social Skills: Does he or she form attachments easily with close relatives or friends? Get along in groups of same-aged children? Seem to understand and be able to play games with rules? Understand what others are feeling and signaling by their actions? Understand body language?_____

_____

_____

Emotional Modulation: How well does the child handle changing emotions and moods? Is he/she generally happy and calm or often agitated and irritable? Easily affected by noisy or hectic situations? How well does he/she put up with frustration? Can he/she calm herself independently after getting upset?_____

_____

_____

Cognitive Ability: How easily does your child learn things compared to others his/her age? Which types of learning (for example, numbers and math, language or reading) seem hardest for him/her?

_____

_____

Motor Skills and Planning: How well does the child move "in space" compared to other children of the same age? How well does he/she run? Does he/she have trouble with skills, such as tying shoes or zipping a coat? Can he/she carry out tasks that include several steps?_____

_____

_____

Step Four: Identify the Top Concerns

Look back at your "Strengths and Concerns" worksheet. Put a checkmark next to your TOP THREE CONCERNS listed on either sheet. These are the things that interfere most with the child's home, school, family, or social life. Knowing which symptoms cause the greatest concern can help your team figure out where to start.

Step Five: Sum Up Strengths and Concerns

In this final step, use your worksheet to describe at least one strength for your child or youth. Then describe the top three concerns in your own words. For example: ("Jared usually tries very hard at all his school activities. But lately he seems tired a great deal but won't talk about it. He's lost weight. He has come home and gone to bed after school every day for the last month.") Try to note where and when the troubling behavior shows up. Is it at family gatherings or at unstructured "hang-out" time with peers? Does it happen during certain seasons or certain times of day, such as bedtime? Does it happen more in public places or during school activities? How long has this behavior gone on?

Make a note of whether the behavior happened during or after a certain event, such as a change at school or a loss in your child's personal life. It is important to be frank about changes in your own life, such as a divorce or loss of a job, that may affect your child's emotions, behavior, and/or daily routine.

Strengths:

	When	Where	How Long
Concern 1:			
Concern 2:			
Concern 3:			

Other issues, comments, or questions:_____

_____

_____

_____

_____

 Brief written information can be very helpful to a provider. However, you can decide whether you would rather give the provider your worksheets or just describe them. It's your choice. However, be sure to hang on to these documents later on. You will want a record of different points along the journey.
Providing information in an organized way tends to make providers treat parents as equal partners. This will be very important as treatment goes on!

Keeping Your Child's Records: Your Child's Health History

Many parents find that a 2-inch, 3-ring binder is the best way to keep paperwork organized and available for appointments, phone calls, and anytime you need to check information. You may want to put a cheap, three-hole-punched calendar (often available at supermarkets, or given away free by many companies) to record appointments and medication dosages. This can be helpful even if you keep appointments on an electronic calendar because sometimes scribbling notes down on a calendar can be a good backup. Try adding tabbed dividers labeled "personal data," "health provider visits," "medications," "evaluations," "school," and "insurance and social agencies."

In the personal data section, include a copy of your child's insurance card, birth certificate, and Social Security card or number (You may wish to "three-hole-punch" a standard business envelope, put it in your binder, and place the Social Security Card inside in order to keep this card number more secure from identity theft.). Add a few sheets of notepaper to each section. Some parents like to put a happy picture of their child or youth on the inside front cover. This reminds everyone (including the parent) to put a "face" on all this treatment talk!

Give Yourself Some Space

It can be very nerve-racking to fill out these forms in 10 or 15 minutes while sitting in a crowded waiting room with a youngster who may need extra attention. Whenever possible, try to have this form mailed to you before the appointment so that you can fill it in on your own time. Often, the physician or other provider's office will have the forms available online.

The space on these forms is usually pretty tight, so if you have more to say, feel free to add extra sheets of paper or write on the reverse side. Write "see over" or "see additional attached notes" on the form, and "Additional notes about (name of your child, date of birth ---)" on any additional pages in case they get separated from the form when office staff put your child's information into their electronic medical records.

Writing the "DOB" (date of birth) on ANY notes written or sent about your child is a good idea because that is one way for the medical office staff to find your child's files in computer systems.

Use the next four pages to keep health information. You can refer to these pages each time you have to fill in a new set of forms. Each provider's form will be a little different, but most will ask for the same basic details. (It is okay to copy this form for your personal use, so you can keep up-to-date information in your binder.)

Label It

Label your binder with your child's name and the year. At the end of the year, put it up on the shelf and start a new binder. This is a convenient way to keep an annual record of your child's treatment. By the time my son David was 20, we had tried 46 different medications. I was glad I had a record! You may want to add a zipper pouch in the front of your binder to keep small items such as prescription receipts, appointment cards, or business cards from providers.

Health History

Date_____

Last Name _____ First name _____ Middle name _____

Gender Identification: Male _____ Female _____ Other _____

Birth Date _____ Where born (city, state, and country) _____

Social Security number _____ Year in school _____ Name of school_____

Primary Language(s) child speaks at home _____

Medical history

Any troubles during pregnancy or birth such as jaundice or premature birth: (If yes, explain)_____

_____

Physical diseases, conditions, or injuries such as juvenile diabetes, anemia, at the present time? Include <u>how long</u> the child has had this condition._____

_____

Physical diseases, conditions, or injuries in the past, with dates if you know them (ex.: seizures, frequent ear infections): _____

Tobacco use in home; substance abuse (see note on page 25):

    Now: _____

    In the past (include when used): _____

Previous substance abuse treatment? _____ If so, when and where? _____

Behavioral health issues already diagnosed (ex.: depression):

Diagnosis: _____ When diagnosed: _____

Any other diagnosis: _____ When diagnosed: _____

Current prescription drugs taken (with dosage):

Medication	Reason for taking	Dosage and instructions

Non-prescription drugs taken (include vitamins, herbs, supplements, and over-the-counter drugs such as cold medicines or pain relievers): _____

Allergies: _____

Drug reactions: _____

Check-ups and routine care	Dates
Last physical examination	
Last eye examination	
Last hearing examination	
Last dental visit	

Immunization ("shot") record. Show latest date given (or get a copy of this record from the child's primary care doctor and keep it with the health history form).

Immunization	Date	Immunization	Date
DTaP (Diphtheria, tetanus, and acellular pertussis):		IPV (Inactive poliovirus)	
PCV (Pneumonia vaccine)		Hepatitis B	
MMR (Measles, mumps, rubella)		Hepatitis C (if given)	
Hib (Influenza vaccine, type b)		Tetanus and diphtheria (if given separately)	
Hepatitis A			

Family Medical History

*Health providers often ask about illnesses in close family members. This is because **genetic traits** (physical and mental qualities you are born with) can lead to certain illnesses that run in families. Knowing that a particular illness has occurred in a close, blood relative may help a doctor determine what's happening to your child or youth. In some cases, a medication that is used to treat an illness in one family member may have a better chance to be successful with another family member. Remember that the genetic traits your child or youth inherited are nobody's fault and nothing that you can control. However, they are very important pieces of information that help fill in the picture for your team. If you have concerns about who will be able to see your personal information, discuss this with the provider who evaluates your child or youth.*

Social History

Child or youth lives with (name): _____

Relationship to child or youth: _____

List information about parents and legal guardians of this child or youth:

Name	Address	Telephone	Relationship	SS#	Date of Birth	Age	Living?

Name and address of employer(s) of parent(s) or guardians(s) _____

_____

_____

_____

Is the child adopted? _____ In foster care? _____

If so, at what age was the child first placed in care? _____

Parents' relationship status: Married _____ Not Married _____ Separated _____ Divorced _____

Currently living in same household? _____ Other _____

Number and ages of child's siblings (brothers and sisters): _____

_____

_____

_____

Relatives or others living with child: _____

_____

_____

_____

Health History, continued

Numbers and ages of siblings not living with child or youth (including step-siblings): _____

_____

_____

Describe any important life events in the past that affect your child's or youth's physical or behavioral health (Ex.: family divorce, major move, tragedy or **trauma**): _____

_____

_____

Family Health History:

Describe any medical, behavioral, or mental health diagnoses in parents, grandparents, or siblings: _____

_____

_____

Describe any unusual, "weird," or negative behavior in close family members. (Example: older brother and father often have sudden rages.) INCLUDE ALCOHOL AND OTHER SUBSTANCE ABUSE. _____

_____

_____

How often does the child get regular exercise? _____

What kind(s) of exercise or sports does the child participate in? _____

Any unusual diet or feeding problems? _____

Other comments about physical, mental, or developmental health (look back at "Your Child's Developmental Profile" on page 19 for other information to add): _____

_____

_____

Developmental Milestones

It can be hard to remember when a child did certain things (especially if the child has been ill or events in the family have been difficult). Sometimes it helps to look at family pictures. This record may also be in your primary care doctor's files. You may need to compare notes with others in the family. That's why it's better to gather this information ahead of time.

Developmental History:

Activity	Age learned
Rolled over without help	
Sat up without support	
Crawled	
Walked	
Ate solid foods	
Fed self with spoon	
Pointed to objects	
Babbled	
Used single words	
Used a string of three words	
Spoke in sentences	

Health History, continued

Mobility, transportation or other adaptive needs (special equipment or procedures for daily living): _____

_____

_____

Doctors, Therapists, and Other Providers:

Name, address, and phone number of primary care doctor or pediatrician:

_____

_____

Specialists

(Name, specialty, address, phone number):

1. _____

_____

2. _____

_____

3. _____

_____

4. _____

_____

Case Manager

Name: _____ Organization: _____

Phone #: _____ Email: _____

Health Insurance

Plan Name: _____ Subscriber ID # _____

Group Policy #: _____ Customer Service phone #: _____

Substance Abuse and Other Behaviors

*It is very important that providers who work with your child know about anything that can affect your child's health, behavior, and emotions. That means knowing about family alcohol and drug abuse, sexual abuse, and any unusual family behaviors or traumas (very negative bad events such as a death, injury, or divorce) that your child has experienced. In most cases, the provider is required to keep this information **confidential** (not telling the police, your employer, or others not involved in the child's treatment) unless the situation will cause a major risk to the child or others. **There are exceptions to this rule.** If you have any questions, talk to the provider about how the information will be used. If you aren't comfortable listing the information on the forms in this book, write it down in a safe place and don't forget to share it with the provider.*

Straight Talk

Guidelines for "screening" (identifying whether a child has a problem that might need further testing) keep changing all the time as new research comes to light. Keep up with the latest at "HealthyChildren.org" from the American Academy of Pediatrics at www.healthy-children.org. One of the most useful tabs is "Ages and Stages."

Making Sense of Reports and Evaluations

The provider who evaluates your child (usually a psychologist or social worker) is sometimes called a **clinician**. This person may use one or more **standardized assessment tools** (often known as tests or **test batteries**) to help **assess** (find out) your child's needs. There are many different types of tests, and in most cases, the clinician must get your written permission to give a test to your child.

Some questions to ask:
1. What is the name of the test?
2. Why is my child being given this test?
3. What kinds of information will this test provide?
4. When will this test be given?
5. How long will the test take?
6. Who will administer (give) the test to my child?
7. When will I receive the results of this test?

Common tests for children include the following:

Cognitive and Adaptive: These types of tests are used to measure the way a child's brain works in terms of intelligence, memory, life skills, attention, use of language, and ways of learning. Some often-used tests in this category include the Woodcock-Johnson, Wechsler Intelligence Scales for Children (WISC), and Vineland Scales of Adaptive Behavior.

Psychological Evaluation: This type of test explores a child's emotional health, social abilities, behavior, and personality. You will usually be asked to fill out a questionnaire about the behavior you see at home. A teacher may also be asked to fill out such a form. (Many of the common symptoms listed on pages 17-18 will appear on this kind of questionnaire.) Some tests in this category include sentence-completion tests, the Children's Depression Inventory, and the Behavioral Assessment System for Children (BASC).

Developmental Evaluation: This kind of test measures a young child's development level compared to same-age children. It measures some of the developmental areas mentioned on page 19. One common test is the Bayley Scales of infant Development.

Educational (or **Psycho-educational**) **Evaluation**: Most often given by the school psychologist, these tests measure intelligence, academic skills, and academic abilities (how the child can and does perform in school compared to others the same age). A psycho-educational evaluation does not diagnose mental illness. School psychologists often use the Woodcock-Johnson, WiSC, and Vineland as well as academic achievement tests.

More About Behavioral Health Providers

The organizations that give health and social services are often called **providers**. Some providers have private practices that employ only one or a few staff members. Some private behavioral health practices are attached to hospitals or clinics. A larger organization that provides behavioral health services may be called a CMHC (Community Mental Health Center), a CMHO Community Mental Health Organization), or CMHA (Community Mental Health Agency). These organizations may employ many psychiatrists, psychologists, social workers, case managers, and support staff.

Choosing Someone to Evaluate Your Child

A primary care provider may refer your child to a specific clinic, doctor or other specialist. The school may suggest that you look for a specialist. Maybe you are concerned about a problem and decide to look for help on your own. You may have to pick someone from the list of providers in your insurance network. In any case, the choice of a clinician is up to YOU.

How do you pick the right person? There are no simple answers. With some types of insurance, you may not need a referral. Call the number on your insurance card if you have questions about this. (See more about insurance in Guiding Star Point 4, "Dealing with Treatment Bills and Benefits.")

Many parents are bothered by the thought of going to someone who will ask them lots of personal questions. It's easy to understand that feeling. This person will ask a lot of questions about your family life. The way you and your child behave toward one another will be observed. The evaluator forms an opinion of your situation from the way you talk to your child, fill out forms, and answer questions.

Look for Clues, Trust Your Instincts

Remember that you also have the right to observe and evaluate the provider who will work with your child. You are hiring that person to do a service for your child. You are seeking help because you need to solve a problem. You can do that best when you feel comfortable giving someone all the necessary information. That means you need someone who knows how to listen. The best clinician will gather the facts and not jump to conclusions. Even the most well-known or recommended person in town may not be right for you or your child. You have to trust your gut instinct. You must notice things, such as body language, that may hint about whether the clinician and your child will get along. Some people like to bring a relative or trusted friend along to the first appointment to get an independent view and have someone to take notes on what was said.

Talking About Therapists

In this book, the word "providers" means people who provide services.

"Clinician" means someone who evaluates your child and may later provide therapy. The term "therapist" usually refers to a psychologist (PhD or PsyD), social worker (LCSW), or licensed counselor who provides "talk therapy." (Such therapy may also involve other methods, such as playing games or doing activities with your child.)

Learn SYSTEM BASICS

David's Story in Ten Photos

Like many children with autism, our son seemed to develop as a typical baby and toddler until 14 months. Then, he stopped babbling and making eye contact. By age 2, he spent most of his time staring into space, never smiling, clutching a favorite toy, and not responding to his own name. Looking back at family photos, it was easy to see a month-by-month decline we didn't notice in "real time." When we began to look for help, I put together ten of these photos to show new providers. It was a quick and dramatic way to communicate his story. (P.S. I am happy to say that the story changed a LOT later on in our journey!)

If you are considering a behavioral health (mental health) clinician who has a private practice, try to talk to this person on the phone first. Ask questions like these:

1. How long have you been in practice?
2. How much of your practice is with children (or youth)? What ages are most of your clients?
3. What type of degrees do you have?
4. Do you have experience working with school systems to get services? Would you be willing to go to a school meeting, if necessary? If so, what kinds of arrangements would I need to make with you? (Most providers will charge for this, and it often will not be covered by insurance.)
5. My child seems to have (explain problem very briefly). How commonly do you see children/youth with this type of problem?
6. Can you please explain what the steps of the evaluation will be? Will you wish to see me for an intake interview separately before you see my child?
7. What sorts of tests do you generally use?
8. What do you charge?
9. Do you file insurance paperwork? What is your procedure for payment?
10. Can I contact you between appointments, if necessary? How do you prefer to be contacted between visits?

Tips for a First Visit

When you see a provider for the first time, pay attention to small cues that could mean a lot. A good clinician will usually begin by asking something such as, "Why are you here?" He or she will clearly explain methods for working together, payment arrangements, and what your role in treatment will be. For example, the clinician might say, "After I meet with your child for about three weeks, I'll want us to get together and review the treatment plan."

The person may want to meet with your child or youth a few times before deciding what, if any, tests to use. If so, you should be given some idea of when to expect this decision. If the child is a teen, the clinician may want to keep some parts of their therapy discussions **confidential** (not telling you). The clinician may do this to build up more trust so the child or youth will be frank and honest in discussions. If that's the case, you should be told clearly in the beginning so you can decide whether to give your **consent** (legally agree to allow this action to happen). You should discuss exactly what kinds of information will and will not be shared.

Pay attention to the person's manner and the office environment. Does the clinician make you and your child or youth feel comfortable? Do you feel your concerns are being heard? If the child or youth has to wait somewhere while you speak to the person privately, is that space safe and comfortable? What does your child or youth think?

If your child or youth receives services from a large agency, one person may conduct the evaluation, and a different person may give therapy. Others, such as a nurse or psychiatrist, may be in charge of medication management. **YOU STILL HAVE A CHOICE.** If one of these persons doesn't seem right to you, you can request someone else. Talk to your case manager if you don't know how to do this. If necessary, ask an administrator within the clinic.

Unfortunately, in some small cities and rural areas there aren't many clinicians, therapists, or psychiatrists. If you really don't think any of the providers seem right for your child, find out whether it's practical to go to a larger city.

Of course, you may need to see the person for more than one visit before you make any judgment. People don't always "click" right away. For more information about this topic, see Guiding Star Point 3, "Working with the Team."

Understanding the Treatment Plan

Once the evaluation process is complete, the clinician will meet with you to develop a treatment plan. This can take several different forms. In some cases, there will be a written report, sometimes called a "Clinical Evaluation Report" or "Clinical Assessment Report." This report will state the reason your child was referred, sum up the child's health history, explain test results, and make recommendations for treatment.

Always be sure the evaluator gives you a dated copy of any report or treatment plan that concerns your child. Often the clinician will go over a "draft" report so you can find any errors. **READ THE REPORT CAREFULLY**. Ask about any results or terms you don't understand. Pay attention to anything in the report about your child's past medications, illnesses, or your family history. Mark your corrections clearly on your copy and file it in your binder. Ask when you can expect to receive a final copy of the report. When you receive it, make sure the corrections were made. Save this copy. If you don't receive it when promised, ask again and keep asking. **It's very important to have an accurate evaluation report because it becomes part of your child's record.** Other providers who treat your child may use parts of it in their own reports. Mistakes may creep in as a "copy of a copy" of your child's records. The real facts can get lost.

Treatment Plan Forms

Large clinics, hospitals, and CMHAs often use a standard form for the treatment plan. Most plans contain this type of information:

STATEMENT OF THE PROBLEM: This part should describe the problem or problems in plain words. It may also include the diagnosis. *Example*: "John is often physically aggressive with children at school. At home, John is observed cycling rapidly between extreme irritation and sadness. Symptoms get worse in winter. Diagnosis: Bipolar disorder with rapid cycling and Seasonal Affective Disorder."

LONG-TERM GOALS: This is how the team pictures a good outcome of treatment. *Example*: "John will learn and practice successful methods for managing anger without aggression. John's moods will be stable enough throughout the year to allow him to function at school and home."

SHORT-TERM GOALS: These are specific goals the team will work on immediately. If possible, there should be some way to measure whether progress to-

Code Words

Clinical evaluation reports often include certain terms that are "shorthand" for things one provider tells another. They might contain sentences such as, "Jane was neatly groomed and appropriately dressed for the season." This means the child seems to be cared for. Tip: If, despite your best efforts, your child shows up at the evaluation very messy, in shoes full of holes or wearing shorts on a freezing day, explain why to the evaluator. ("I know it looks strange, but wearing long pants makes him have a meltdown.") If the hot water failed that morning and nobody could take a shower, explain this. Don't be embarrassed, just frank. Remember, the clinician isn't a mind reader; he or she knows the situation is difficult for you. Full information can only help.

En Su Lengua

La mayoría de las organizaciones grandes de salud harán el intento de traducir en su idioma (POR ESCRITO) el plan de tratamiento si usted no lee inglés adecuadamente. Solicite este servicio si lo necesita. Es importante que usted entienda el plan para que pueda consentir al mismo y se pueda involucrar debidamente.

ward the goals is being made. These goals should include a date to review whether the plan is working. *Example*: "Episodes of physical aggression will be decreased by at least one outburst weekly. John will show increased mood stability over a period of one month. Review progress with parent after one month from start of treatment." (Remember: These are goals, not promises. It's hard to predict whether or how soon a person's behavior will change.)

INTERVENTION PLAN: This plan describes actions people on the team will take to help your child or youth reach the goals. An intervention plan should always list what will be done, who will do it, and how often actions will happen. It should list a start date and an estimated date to complete or review the actions. ***The plan should also include what you and other family members will do.*** *Example*:

a. "Medications to be prescribed by Doctor A for aggression and mood stability. Weekly medication management by Nurse B until John is stable for one month. Review medication as needed.

b. Psychotherapy sessions with MSW Therapist C twice weekly.

c. Family therapy session with C every two weeks.

d. Team meeting with parents in one month or sooner, if needed."

CRISIS PLAN: If your child's or youth's condition poses a threat to him or her self, the family, or others, this part should describe what steps will be taken if things get a lot worse. The plan should tell you whom to contact first, such as the number of the local Mental Health Crisis or Specialized Crisis Services, which hospital will accept your child in a crisis, and who will communicate with the hospital. Sometimes this plan is put on another form. Make sure it includes all necessary phone numbers.

OTHER INFORMATION AND NEEDS: If your child or youth has special needs that affect the plan (such as a medical condition or disability), this should be stated on the treatment plan.

You and all members of the treatment team who will provide services should sign this plan. If you don't agree with something on the plan, state what the problems are and discuss them. Ask about alternatives. Remember to put a copy of this treatment plan in your binder.

A Note About Private Clinicians. Sometimes a clinician will prefer to see your child or youth for a while before developing a treatment plan. Some providers (especially those in private practice) don't use written treatment plans. This may be okay. You have to judge whether it's comfortable for you. However, getting a plan on paper ensures there are fewer misunderstandings. Also, it provides a way to see if progress is being made. In addition, it includes estimated times to review and change treatment. You can send copies to your primary care provider and school to keep them informed.

If your clinician or case manager doesn't offer any form of treatment plan, ask why not. If you would prefer to have one, say so.

Getting Medication Facts

If medication is part of your child's or youth's treatment plan, here are some questions you might ask the doctor or nurse:

1. How will this medication help my child?
2. How commonly is the medication used in children of this age?
3. How much experience do you personally have with prescribing this medication? Is this a brand-name medication? Is it available in a less expensive generic version?
4. What is the name of the generic version? Can we use it?
5. Can we switch between brands or between the generic and the brand-name medicine?
6. What is the dosage? Is it likely to change during the time my child is getting used to it? Will my child need a different dosage as she grows?
7. What if my child can't swallow a pill or capsule? Is it available in chewable form?
8. How many times each day must the medicine be taken? What time of day?
9. Does this medication need to be taken with food?
10. Who will monitor (keep track of) my child's medications?
11. Will my child need any laboratory tests with this medication? If so, how often?
12. Does my child need to avoid any foods when taking this medication?
13. What are possible side effects? Which ones are most likely?
14. Which side effects mean that I should contact your office immediately?
15. How shall I contact you if a worrisome side-effect occurs? (Tip: Write down the phone number and a contact name. Ask if there is a "patient portal," which is an online way to contact your provider's office and/or keep medical records.)
16. If you are not available, whom should I call?
17. What if my child skips a dose or spits it up?
18. Should I check in with your office before the next appointment to let you know how the medication is working? If so, when and how?

Source: Linda Zweifel, Former Director of Programs, NAMI Montgomery County, Texas

More About Behavioral Health Medications

Psychiatric medications are drugs used for behavioral health problems such as mood or thought disorders (for example, depression and schizophrenia). Sometimes these are called psychotropic or psychoactive medications. Most of the psychiatric medications prescribed for younger children are prescribed **off-label**, which means the United States Food and Drug Administration (FDA) has not yet approved these drugs to be used for that age group. So far, the FDA has conducted very few tests of medications for children's behavioral disorders.

Doctors use their own experience, as well as the experience of other doctors and researchers, to determine which drugs work best in each situation. As with adults, medications don't work the same for different children. The doctor may have

Fast Facts

The American Academy of Child & Adolescent Psychiatry answers common questions about medications in its "Facts for Families" guides. It contains information in several languages, and special topics of interest to groups such as military families and gay, lesbian, bisexual, and transgender youth. Go to www.aacap.org/AACAP/ Families_and_ Youth/ Facts_for_Families.

Medline Plus

The website www.medline-plus.gov, a service of the National Library of Medicine and the National Institutes of Health, covers hundreds of health topics and medications. You'll find plain-spoken information about drug interactions and current warnings. Also included is an encyclopedia of medical terms, current news about health risks, and links to many other useful sites.

to try several drugs or combinations of drugs. It may take several tries to get the right **dosage** (amount of the drug).

What to Know about Drug Warnings

New information about medications is always appearing.

Sometimes a drug will be given a **black-box warning** by the FDA, telling doctors to be careful about using the drug under certain conditions. A black-box warning doesn't necessarily mean the drug is dangerous under all conditions. Sometimes warnings are about not using certain drugs for certain disorders. Sometimes they warn about **drug interactions**, which means possible problems when one drug is used at the same time as another drug. Other warnings are for dangerous side effects that may (but don't always) occur. There are hundreds of drugs that can affect one another.

Frankly, doctors are only human and may not always be aware of certain interactions or side effects. An extra pair of eyes on the task never hurts and often helps. You'll also know what side effects or danger signs to look for so you can report them to the doctor right away. (See also "*Get to Know Your Pharmacist,*" page 39.)

Preventing Confusion About Drug Samples

Sometimes the doctor will **titrate** a new medication (build up from a smaller to a larger dose over a period of days or weeks). This is done in order to find out what amount works best or to cut down on possible side effects. Some medications need to build up in the body over days or weeks in order to be effective. In a crisis situation, a doctor may prescribe an extra medication (for a short time) to keep symptoms under control, until another medication has time to build up to a **therapeutic dose** (an amount that is effective for the child or youth).

If a new medication is being tried (especially if the medication is expensive), the provider may start you with free samples. He or she may say something like "Give her 10 milligrams for the first three days, then raise it to 20 milligrams for a week, then call and let me know how it's going." The trouble is that a sample package does not have your child's dosage on the label the way a regular prescription would. It's easy to get confused, especially when you are changing the dosage from day to day.

Ask the provider to write down instructions for titrating medications. If you're getting a prescription, ask the doctor to write titration instructions on the prescription form. This will help to ensure that you get the right number of pills from the pharmacy. See Guiding Star Point 4, "Tracking Your Child's Progress," for an easy way to keep up with titration changes and to record the results.

Medication Abbreviations

Here are some abbreviations you might find on prescription forms, on orders for lab tests, and in your child's or youth's medical files:

b.i.d.   give medication twice a day

CBC   complete blood count

ECG   electrocardiogram (looks for heart problems)

EEG   electro-encephalogram (looks for brainproblems)

g   gram (unit of measurement)

h.s.   at bedtime

kg   kilogram

L   liter

mg   milligram

NSAID   Non-steroidal anti-inflammatory drug (such as aspirin)

O2   oxygen

OTC   over-the-counter (non-prescription)

P.O.   by mouth

P.R.   rectally (in the child's bottom)

p.r.n.   as needed

q   every day

q.i.d.   four times a day

RBC   red blood-cell count

S.L.   sublingual (under the tongue)

t.i.d.   three times a day

WBC   white blood-cell count

Source: Linda Zweifel, Former Director of Programs, NAMI Montgomery County, Texas. Used with author's permission.

Keeping It Simple

We had to try a lot of different medications to get the right combination for David, so we ended up juggling a lot of drug samples over the years. After a while, I wrote the dosage directions on the sample box (one tablet on Tuesday 3/5, two tablets on Wednesday 3/6, etc.) so I didn't get mixed up. I also used the calendar system described in Guiding Star Point 4, "Tracking Your Child's Progress."

Guiding Star Point Three: Build RELATIONSHIPS

There Are No Stupid Questions

Remember to ask:
- *Who?*
- *What?*
- *When?*
- *Where?*
- *Why?*
- *How?*
- *Can You Explain?*

And write down the answers whenever possible!

Working with the Team

As a parent, you are responsible for making sure that the providers on your child's team work together. That means you also have the right to be treated as a full partner. Even a good provider can get too busy, feel cranky, or jump to conclusions. If this happens all the time, you may need to find someone else. However, a good provider is more likely to treat you as an equal partner *if you show confidence in yourself.* It doesn't matter if you don't have all the answers. Nobody does.

However, each time you walk into a room to deal with a provider, remember: *As the parent of that child, YOU are in a position of authority, too.* These "family-tested" tips are adapted from advice for parents from Tennessee Voices for Children, a parent support and advocacy organization:

1. *You have a right to be treated with courtesy and respect.* Everyone responds better if they are treated respectfully. You, the parent, know the most about your child. It's not acceptable for you to be treated as less than an equal.

2. *If you don't know how the provider came to a conclusion, ask for an explanation.* A recommendation will always make more sense if you see clearly what led to it. Continue to ask questions until you understand the provider's thinking. *You may disagree with providers about their recommendations for your child.* Don't be afraid to say so. Providers aren't perfect. Sometimes they are mistaken. You know your child in a way they can't. If you think what they're suggesting won't work for your child, say so. Based on your input, providers may change their recommendations.

3. *Explain your point of view in a calm, courteous way.* Don't attack the provider just because you don't agree. If you are calm rather than angry when expressing your opinion, the provider will be much more likely to see you as a partner who has a different point of view rather than as a "difficult parent." It's okay to disagree, to express emotion, cry, or be angry, but if you are feeling out of control, ask for a short break to gather yourself. You might also end early and schedule another meeting.

4. *If you need more time with the provider, say so.* If your appointment isn't long enough to get all your questions answered, the provider should be willing to schedule more time to meet with you. You are entitled to this. It may mean having to set another meeting on another day, but you have a right to get complete, clear information about your child.

5. ***Keep in regular contact with any provider involved with your child.*** In some instances, it's important to see a provider on a regular basis if you are going to get the best for your child. Check with providers to see how often they recommend that you talk to them.

6. ***Encourage members of your child's team to talk with one another.*** Part of your job as the coach of your child's team is to make sure the team members are all communicating. (See below for for more tips on how to keep all the team members informed.)

7. ***If you are pleased with a provider, say so.*** Just like everyone else, providers like to know when they are doing a good job. A simple "thank you" can mean a lot and will go a long way toward guaranteeing that they continue to do the best job they can.

8. ***If you can't work things out with a provider directly, you may need to discuss your problems with a supervisor.*** Make sure you've made every effort to resolve things with the provider before you see a supervisor.

9. ***If you have tried all the above and still cannot get along with the provider, think about changing to a different person.*** Sometimes people simply cannot get along. If you have done the best you can and still do not feel comfortable with the provider, you'll be better off finding someone else to help your family.

Adapted from: "Working with Professionals" by Tennessee Voices for Children. Used with permission.

How to Keep the Whole Team Informed

Picture your team standing in a circle. In the middle of that circle: you and your child. Say that one team member has an important piece of information they all should know. Let's call it the ball. Some parts of the team have a system for passing this "ball" back and forth. The process occurs most easily when they work for the same organization. However, doctors, therapists, and case managers may also need to communicate with insurance plans, social agencies, and schools.

That's one reason why you have to sign all those "**permission to release information**" forms. (Learn more about these forms in "The Classroom-Treatment Connection" chapter).

However, many parents are surprised at how often they need to catch that ball and send it on to others. Here's an example of what can happen when a parent doesn't act to keep information flowing:

Let's say a child is showing new symptoms. The psychiatrist and parent agree to a medication change. However, nobody tells the primary care doctor. The psychiatrist doesn't know that the primary care doctor just gave medication for the child's winter ear infection. The two drugs may affect one another, but neither doctor is aware of it.

Hitting the Pause Button

I'll never forget David's first kindergarten IEP meeting. I felt so alone in a room filled with ten school staff and specialists. The school psychologist began a long explanation of David's problems, using test scores that made no sense to me. I could feel my eyes welling up. "Excuse me," I gasped, "I'm having an allergy attack!" I dashed out of the room, made it to a stall in the teacher's lounge, and broke down in sobs. Then I threw cold water on my face, blotted off with scratchy brown paper towels, took a deep breath, and went back to the meeting. Just that little bit of "losing it" gave me the strength to carry on.

Build RELATIONSHIPS

Passing the Ball

Providers need the right information at the right time. Our health system and pure human error often put barriers in the way. It's up to you to keep the right information bouncing among the members of your child's treatment team. The methods in this chapter can make passing that ball a lot easier.

Meanwhile, the teacher notices the child is very sleepy in class. She hasn't been told this could be a side effect of the new medication. She thinks maybe his mother isn't getting him to bed on time. Nobody at the school calls his therapist or psychiatrist to say the child's grades are sliding downhill. The therapist may not know that school troubles are making the child feel more discouraged. Of course, neither the therapist nor psychiatrist has told the school about the new symptoms (which is why the child is taking those medications that make him sleepy). Although all the providers in this example are doing their jobs, they aren't able to pass along all of the information. The result is that nobody has all the facts they need to help that child.

Watch Out for Common System Errors

The example above doesn't even include all those very common moments when the regular communication system breaks down. Sometimes important lab results don't show up before your child's next appointment. The referral phone call never gets made. A phone message gets mangled on its way between offices. Human errors will always happen, but a few tricks can help the information get where it needs to go.

One rule of thumb: If you can cut out a step that somebody else normally does, you can cut down the number of times it gets done wrong. *Example*: On some health forms and laboratory paperwork, you are asked to list doctors that should be informed. **Make sure to have the names and contact information for providers who should get copies.** If office staff members have to look up the information, the task may get put on the "hold" pile until someone has spare time.

Next, find out when the results will be ready. If the doctor needs them soon, call the office on that day to see if the results have been received. If the results have not shown up, your call will remind the staff to call and ask the lab about them. Before your child's next visit, check to see if the test results have arrived.

Often there is only space for two or three names on that list of contacts, and sometimes the office will send results only to specialists involved in your child's care. (Remember, they may not be able to send your child's records to other providers without a signed release from you.) If you want schools, therapists, or others on the team to be informed, it may be easiest to send or bring copies yourself. You are the only one who always has permission to release information.

Passing Notes, Patient Portals

Always ask for a copy of any report or lab result. YOU HAVE A RIGHT TO GET A COPY OF ALL DOCUMENTS ABOUT YOUR CHILD. Medical records are now electronic (in a computer), but the office should make you a paper copy. Save this in your binder. (Some people prefer to keep all records on their tablets or phones. That is your choice, but paper is always a safe backup!) If there is something in this report that another team member should know, write a note or email (if he or she is a provider) to put the information in the child's file.

Whenever possible, WRITE the information--don't just tell it to the person. Information gets lost, forgotten or misunderstood. Plus, you may need a record later. Email is best because you have a record of what you wrote. If you are not sure about what to include, ask the provider to help you before you leave the appointment. If writing is difficult for you, find out if you can get a case manager or an advocate from a local family organization to help you. Try calling 211 on the phone or visit 211.org online to ask about resources for families with special physical, mental health, or developmental needs.

Many health providers now use a **patient portal** to keep records and exchange information with patients and family caregivers. In this system, you can sign into a personal account that lets you find information, set up or cancel appointments, and send messages to your health provider. If your pediatrician or other health provider offers this system, sign up. If it seems confusing, ask someone in the provider's office to help you during the next appointment. This is one more reason to keep a good relationship with provider support staff! They usually know better than anyone else how their systems work.

Who Needs What

The need for a regular information exchange will vary according to who's on your team and what they need. Ask each team member, "Whom do you usually notify about a change in my child's treatment? Would you like to be notified when someone else makes a change? How would you like to get this information? Should I send it to you for my child's file? Should I just bring it the next regular appointment?"

Here are some general guidelines for keeping the providers on your team informed of important changes:

For a **MEDICATION CHANGE**, tell:
- Other doctors
- Therapists
- Case Manager
- School personnel (This may include the teacher, counselor, or school nurse, even if your child does not take these medications at school. Be sure to advise them about possible side effects, such as sleepiness or excessive thirst so they can keep you informed. When they tell you something you think is important, keep health providers informed.)
- Church or after-school youth group leaders

Forms, Forms, Forms
The **Health Insurance Portability and Accountability Act (HIPAA)** *requires health providers to get your consent before releasing information under certain conditions. In general, you will have to sign a release every time information is sent from one organization (such as your doctor's office) to another organization (such as the insurance plan administrators). If you don't understand who will get this information and for what reason, don't sign until you get the answers.*

Build RELATIONSHIPS

Keep Siblings in Mind

Changes in your child or youth's condition may also affect siblings (brothers and sisters) or other children living in the home. Your child or youth's privacy is important, but teachers and school staff who care for other children in the family often need to know about situations that may cause symptoms to appear. Sometimes a child can be very "good" and cooperative at home when a family is dealing with another child's problems, but may show symptoms of anger or depression at school. Sometimes the distress shows up as physical problems such as headaches or stomachaches. Teachers and school staff can be your "eyes and ears" to alert you about these issues before they become big problems. For more about coping with family challenges, see Guiding Point Five: Finding SUPPORT.

- Parent who does not have custody (under the legal agreement)
- Other or adoptive foster parent, if more than one
- Childcare staff or other caregivers

For a **TREATMENT PLAN CHANGE**, tell:
- All doctors
- Other therapists
- School staff (such as classroom teacher), if needed
- Others who observe the child's behavior (such as paid caregivers, babysitters, after-school care staff)

For a **MAJOR LIFE EVENT** (such as a trauma), tell:
- All major team members
- Others who care for your child or youth.

NOTE: Your child or youth (and family) has a **right to privacy**, but it may be very important for others (such as a babysitter or parent of a child's playmate) to know what's happening. Sometimes this can be a tough call. Consider talking this over with providers on your team, including your child or youth.

Tips for Sending Updates

An update note doesn't have to be formal or complicated. The important points to include:
- Key facts (what happened, what changed, such as a medication change, treatment plan change, etc.)
- Your child's date of birth
- When this happened
- Who is involved (for example, what provider made the change) and this person's role
- What paperwork is included with this note, if any (such as a lab or test result)
- Any additional information
- Where you can be reached if a release form is needed.

If you are sending this note to a provider, it helps to add: "Please include this information in my child's file, and contact me if you need further information. Thank you for helping to keep my child's records up to date."

Get to Know Your Pharmacist

A good pharmacist could be your single best source of information about medications. Most are willing to spend time making sure you have all the facts. Pharmacists also know a lot about your prescription drug insurance.

Use the same pharmacy location. If that's not possible, use the same chain. The stores in one chain will usually have the same computer system to hold patient information. If your insurance requires you to use a "mail-order" pharmacy, there is usually a toll-free number to call with questions. Look on the bottle or in the packaging that comes with the child's medications. Always check the label on the medicine bottle to make sure the details match the prescription form. If the doctor sends the information to the pharmacy electronically without giving you a prescription form, ask for a copy of the form before you leave. Pharmacists may substitute the less expensive "generic" for a brand-name drug. That's fine so long as the doctor has not marked "name brand only" on the prescription. Also, look at the drug information inside the prescription envelope, medicine box, or flyer.

Ask about anything you don't understand. Check for stickers on the bottle that give warnings such as "take with food" or "avoid sun exposure," and ask for more details. (What kind of food? Can I give this an hour after my child eats? My child plays on a team outdoors. If I put a strong sunscreen on him, is that good enough? What does "drink plenty of water" really mean?)

Ask about side effects, even if the doctor has already mentioned them. A busy doctor may not tell you everything (or know everything) about a medication. Ask which side effects mean you should check back with the pharmacy or doctor right away. Unlike health practices, pharmacies usually can answer questions on nights and weekends and will get right on the phone with you. Often, they can also call the doctor's office directly and get answers more quickly.

Be sure your child's pharmacy record includes any over-the-counter (non-prescription) drugs your child takes. Ask about meds for temporary illnesses, such as colds, infections, or viruses. If, for some reason, the pharmacist is not helpful with answering questions, think about using a different pharmacy. If a "mail order" pharmacy assistant is not helpful, ask to speak with a supervisor.

Take time to form a good relationship with your pharmacist. Plan ahead to get refills. Use automated refill phone lines and automatic refill reminder systems if they are offered. Ask what times of the day or week the store is busiest. Try not to call with questions or prescription needs during "rush" hours, so the pharmacist can give you the attention you need.

Meds Safety

See Guiding Star Point 4, "Tracking Your Child's Progress," for more tips on organizing medications, observing side effects, and keeping track of behavior changes.

Build RELATIONSHIPS

Amazing but True

The busy doctor who seems to rush you out the door all the time will almost always stop and listen IF you bring along a written list of questions. The key is a written list. For some reason, this tactic is not as effective if the questions aren't written down on an actual piece of paper or in a notebook. The paper itself seems to provide a visual cue to pay attention! Refer to the list when speaking. For example, you might say, "Let's see–I have just two more questions here." This is a well-tested method for getting a provider to slow down and provide the information you need. Also, doctors and clinicians respect a parent who seems organized and who expects a full response.

Making the Most Of Appointment Time

1. ***Be on time for the appointment.*** If you have to cancel, give 24 hours' notice whenever possible. Some offices charge for appointments that are cancelled without notice, and insurance companies don't pay for that charge. Take along the office number. If you are stuck in traffic and have a cell phone, call and tell them the reason you might be late. Most offices will give you a 15-minute "grace period." If you are later than this, they may ask you to reschedule.

2. ***Before each appointment, make a written list of what you need to tell or ask the provider.*** Be brief and stick to the point. Take out your list and refer to it as you speak. Put the most important matters first.

3. ***Know your own listening style.*** Some people find that jotting down what the other person says helps them focus better. However, if writing things down will distract you, consider bringing someone else along to take notes.

4. ***Repeat what the provider says in your own words.*** (This is known as "mirroring" or making a "Reflective Response.") You might say:
   • In other words, do you mean...
   • So, what you're saying is...
   • As I understand it, you mean...
   • Am I correct that you want...
     Just let me make sure I've got this right...
   • Then you would agree that...
   This gives the team member a chance to correct or add to the explanation. Don't be embarrassed if you heard imperfectly. The provider wants you to understand his or her recommendations.

5. ***Before you leave, do an "exit check."*** Check that the provider has given you all necessary prescriptions or copies of the prescriptions sent electronically, plus medicine samples, instructions, and paperwork. Make sure you have placed these things in a safe spot. Many things are forgotten in the last rush of a short appointment. Get into the habit of doing this "exit check" before you leave.

Keeping an Eye on "The Big Picture"

Even the best providers can sometimes lose track of "The Big Picture" of your child's or youth's goals. As you work with providers, think about whether the treatment your child or youth is receiving seems to be meeting the goals and objectives listed in your child's or youth's treatment plan. Ask questions. Do these goals still make sense based on what YOU observe about your child or youth? Treatment plans are "living documents" that can be changed as needed.

Waiting Room Survival Tactics

For families with younger children, a 30-minute wait in the outer office can seem endless. Plan to bring some favorite books or small toys to keep youngsters occupied. Check out the room on the first appointment so you can get prepared for next time. Is there somewhere your child can have a healthy snack while waiting? Is it possible for your child to play a little outside before going in? Is there a convenient restroom to visit before you enter?

If waiting is a big problem, discuss this with the provider. Finding ways for your child to improve "waiting" behavior can sometimes become part of the treatment plan. Two ideas:

1. One parent who worked long hours made a deal with her six-year-old that waiting-room minutes would be their "special time" to read, color, play a game, or talk together. The child started to look forward to these times, and waiting-room behavior improved.

2. Many offices that cater to children play animated (cartoon) movies in the waiting room. This can be a good way to keep kids occupied UNLESS your child is very unhappy about being interrupted when it's time to go into an examining room. One family's tip: Ask the reception staff to shut off the player until your child leaves the room. They can be very helpful about this. Nobody wants a noisy meltdown, any more than you do!

Rehearsing the proper waiting-room behavior with your child can make a difference. ("In the waiting room, we keep an inside voice. You need to sit quietly in a chair and look at your book. When the nurse calls us, you'll put the toys away. Then we'll walk into the doctor's office, and you'll go sit in the brown chair.") Rehearse the same behavior every time you visit the office. Possibly offer a small reward or privilege for following your rules. Again, try to get paperwork done ahead of time so you won't need to fill it out while keeping an eye on your child.

Bear in mind that a waiting room is not a good place for a "showdown" with your child. Yelling at, swatting, or spanking your child will not do much good. Also, it may not give the providers in that office a positive view of your parenting skills. Try to stay cool.

Be honest with the provider and staff about difficulties. Mention what works in other situations. They see this kind of thing all the time, and your conversation may spark some good ideas. Remember, this is just one more problem to be solved by cooperation between you and your team.

Cell Updates

One mother of a child with severe ADHD would sometimes call ahead to see how late the doctor was running that day. If he was 30 minutes behind schedule, the receptionist gave the mother permission to arrive a bit later. The father of a child with autism would wait in the car with his son, letting him play with a favorite toy. The receptionist would call the father's cell phone when the doctor was ready, so they were able to walk right in. A good relationship with office staff made their lives much easier!

Build RELATIONSHIPS

Getting Help From Advocacy Groups

Family advocacy organizations *can help with advice or letter-writing. In some cases, a member of an organization will go with you to a meeting or appointment. One of the most useful family advocacy organizations is the National Alliance on Mental Illness (NAMI), which has affiliate groups all over the nation. Many NAMI affiliates also offer free classes and support groups for parents. Go to www.nami.org to find the closest affiliate.*

Another excellent source of help are chapters of the National Federation of Families for Children's Mental Health. Go to www.ffcmh.org to find one near you.

What to Do When Someone's Not Listening

Problems happen. People don't always get along. You may be denied services or feel your views are not being heard. Whatever the situation, it's up to you to act like an equal partner on the team who deserves ***respect*** and ***results***. Here are some suggestions from the Tennessee Mental Health Consumers' Association:

Approaches that are likely to work:

- Understand that mental health providers are only human. They will do what they can; you do what you can.
- Learn what services you can expect from your providers.
- Learn about agency grievance procedures. (Note: These are steps you have to take when making a formal complaint about a provider or about the services you receive.)
- Learn about the services and resources available in your community.
- If you have a complaint, keep a written record of what happened. Include dates, names of those involved, witnesses, and specific details.
- Go to the person who can make the decision you are asking for. If a problem cannot be resolved on one level, take it to the next.
- Be polite, but keep asking until you are satisfied.

Tips for Success:

- If you have a problem with a provider, first talk to him or her about it before going to someone higher up in the agency.
- Listen to the provider all the way through, just as you like to be heard.
- Politely insist that the provider listen to you all the way through. Give details to back up your points.
- If the problem is resolved, thank the provider.
- If you are not satisfied, take your concern to the next level. Keep going up the chain of command until you are satisfied.
- If you are still not satisfied, file a written **grievance** (letter) with the agency, government mental health authority, or behavioral health organization. You have a right to a copy of the results of each grievance.
  Contact an advocacy organization to help you.

Reprinted from BRIDGES: A Peer-Taught Curriculum on Recovery from Mental Illness by Sita Diehl, MSSW, Barbara A Nelson, and Elizabeth Baxter, MD. Reprinted with permission from NAMI Tennessee and Tennessee Mental Health Consumers' Association.

Practicing Assertiveness

The way you speak, move, dress, and react can affect how you are treated by providers. Assertiveness experts offer these tips on getting results at an appointment or meeting:

Project the right image.

- Dress neatly.
- Greet people firmly. Make strong eye contact.
- Take time to organize records and paperwork.
- Sit or stand in an upright but relaxed way. Keep your body still and relaxed. Fidgeting will make you seem uneasy or lacking in confidence.
- If you feel nervous, practice what you want to say ahead of time.

Speak with confidence.

- State clearly and calmly what you believe to be true ("I think that... I feel that...").
- Speak up in a strong tone of voice without asking for permission or making apologies.
- Don't try to attack, bully, blame, or shame the other person. Your goal is to solve problems, not win arguments.
- Listen to the other person carefully. Show you are listening by wearing an alert, attentive expression.
- Refer to the other person's point of view when you give a different opinion ("I understand that you feel...but I believe...").
- When you honestly agree with the person, say so. A little stroking never hurts ("Yes, that seems like a good idea.").
- Don't raise your voice. If you aren't satisfied, say so politely but firmly. Make suggestions. Ask for ideas.

Show you expect results.

- Before you leave the room, briefly sum up the discussion, describing what each person has agreed to do.
- State decisions in terms of "we" and "us" ("So, as I understand it, we've decided to..."). Remember, you are the other vote in the room.
- If you think the other person may not clearly understand or stick to the agreement, send a note that sums up the decisions made in your meeting. Keep a copy for your files. In case of a conflict, this letter becomes part of the record to help you get results.

Learn More

The Mouse, the Monster and Me: Assertiveness for Young People by Pat Palmer Ed.D., author; Louise Hart, Ed.D., editor; Sue Rama (illustrator). This is a delightful little book that conveys ideas about assertive behavior to young children. It's never too early to start teaching children to express themselves calmly but firmly, particularly when talking about their own treatment needs. A good resource for the waiting room! Find it at www.amazon.com.

Guiding Star Point Four: Manage INFORMATION

Be Good to Yourself

*Sometimes parents of children with behavioral health problems can get very worn out and overwhelmed. A different system can help. Talking to other parents in the same situation can help. The important thing to remember is that you are not a failure because things aren't working out. **See Guiding Star Point 5: Find SUPPORT** for more on how to cope.*

Tracking Your Child's Progress

4.1: Medical/Behavioral Treatment. As a parent, you serve as the eyes and ears of the treatment team. For a "medication management" visit, your child may spend as little as 15 minutes once every few weeks with a psychiatrist or nurse. A physical therapy session may be less than an hour once per week.

These providers have a lot of knowledge about why children behave the way they do and how certain behaviors can change, but you are the one who can tell what your child is doing most of the time. You are the best one to gather this information from other caregivers, such as your child's teacher, other relatives, youth-group leader, or childcare staff. Your jobs as the parent observer on this team are to:

1. Give medications in a safe, organized way.

2. Observe how the treatment affects your child's behavior in everyday life.

3. Watch for any danger signs and take prompt action to get help.

4. Report facts clearly to the treatment team.

For a busy parent with a difficult child, all of these tasks can seem impossible. What if you make a mistake with medication? How do you know what side effects to look for? Who has time to write down all the details of a child's behavior when every day is a new struggle? What if you just aren't a very organized person?

The good news: You don't have to be neat, organized, or any kind of expert to do the tasks listed above. The best tips and tools for doing this job come from parents who don't have time and patience for a lot of paperwork.

The most important tool or a busy parent to have is a regular routine that ***FITS YOUR PERSONAL STYLE.*** Everybody functions better when a few things are done the same way every day. We are more likely to stick with routines that are so simple we don't even need to remind ourselves to do them after a while. You probably have some of these routines in your life already. Maybe you can do certain things when you get up in the morning, right after a meal, or just before bed.

How to Be a Good Recorder

The key is to link this parent record-keeping routine with other natural routines in your life. That way, when the unexpected happens, you are more likely to go back to these tasks.

For example, let's say that after your kids are in bed, you take time to relax for a little while and have a snack. Then you get things ready for the next day. You decide that after you relax for a bit and before you start preparing for the next day, you'll pull out the binder (or go to the computer) and make a few notes about your child. Maybe you decide to spend 10 minutes updating some of the worksheets in this chapter. If you do it every school night, that's all the time it takes. If you miss a few nights because something else happened, you go back to this habit when you can return to the regular routine.

Keep your routine simple and short. Give yourself time to get used to it and don't feel guilty if it doesn't always work. Many parents like to attach the check-in routine to something pleasant, like having that snack, drinking a cup of coffee, or sitting in front of the TV set.

Also, it's a good idea to make sure materials, such as your binder and a pencil or pen, are stored in the same convenient place so you don't have to use that check-in time to hunt for what you need.

Avoiding Medication Mix-ups

A good routine is the key to giving medications safely. Here are some "family-tested/provider approved" strategies for making sure medications stay organized:

- If your child takes regular doses of more than one drug, keep these medications sorted in a seven-day pill organizer. Buy this small, inexpensive plastic box at any pharmacy. The organizer makes it much easier to give meds accurately on a busy school morning when everybody is rushing out the door.
- You can send the box along when the child goes to stay with other relatives or caregivers. Also, you can see at a glance if a dose has been missed.
- Put vitamins and other **over-the-counter medicines** (non-prescription medicines) your child takes in the same box.
- **GIVE THE EXACT DOSAGE.** If the medication comes in liquid form, use a special measuring tool, such as a medication cup, spoon, dropper, or a syringe. Sometimes the tool comes with the medication. Ask the pharmacist about the best tool to use.
- If you have to split pills, you may want to buy an inexpensive pill-cutter from the pharmacy.
- Don't split pills unless the doctor says this is okay. Some pills cannot be split safely.

Pill Refill Routine

Refill the pill organizer on the same day each week. This is a good time to check the front of the bottle for the number of refills left. Check the dosage, too. Use the Medication Log on page 48 to cut down on mistakes. Also, some pharmacies offer pills already sorted into daily "blister packs." (They may charge a fee if your insurance does not cover this service.) If a child is on several medications, this can be a wonderful time-saver and prevent mistakes.

Manage INFORMATION

Lock 'Em Up

The safest way to store medications is in a locked box or cabinet. You can buy this kind of box at most discount or hardware stores. Some health and social services agencies require parents to keep medications locked up.

Medication Safety Tips

1. **STORE MEDICATIONS AT THE RIGHT TEMPERATURE.** Many drugs are sensitive to heat and may become less effective. Some parents keep a small container with extra meds in a purse or car. If so, make sure the meds are securely stored and don't get overheated.

2. **STORE MEDICATIONS IN A SAFE PLACE.** If young children are in the house, use childproof caps.

3. **NEVER** give more or less medication than the doctor prescribes.

4. **NEVER** stop giving a medication without talking to the doctor.

5. **ASK THE DOCTOR OR PHARMACIST** what to do if a dose is missed or spit up. Follow these instructions carefully.

6. **KNOW WHAT TO DO IN CASE OF AN ACCIDENTAL OVERDOSE.** If the child doesn't show immediate symptoms of illness, call your pharmacy or local Poison Control number. In a crisis situation, call 911 for help, and ask to be connected to Poison Control for more advice until help arrives.

7. **LET OLDER CHILDREN SHARE RESPONSIBILITY FOR MEDICATIONS.** It's a good idea for older teens who are medically stable to begin learning how to take and keep track of their own medications. They will need this skill as young adults. However, just like learning to drive or manage money, this is a transition that must be carefully supervised by parents. Talk to your child's doctor and therapist about how and when to start this process. Encourage your child to use the check-off worksheets in this chapter.

8. **PREVENT TEEN PRESCRIPTION DRUG ABUSE.** Teens should not have access to medicines they don't take. Keep these out of sight and reach. Many young people will experiment by helping themselves to prescription drugs in the house. This is a growing problem that can lead to injury and death. Talk to your child about this issue. Watch out for peers who may look for prescription drugs in your house or influence your child to do so.

9. **KEEP TRACK OF MEDICATION DOSES TO PREVENT "PILL HOARDING."** This is a situation in which a child or youth doesn't take (or pretends to take) medications, and then saves them to be shared with others or used in an inappropriate way (such as an overdose attempt).

10. **MOST OF ALL,** if your child is severely depressed or at risk of self-injury, lock up all medications. An overdose of the drugs could be used on impulse with tragic results. If you don't know whether this is a concern, talk to your doctor.

Keeping a Titration Record

If a medicine is being titrated (gradually increased over days or weeks), you will need to keep the dosage straight and observe results. Here is a five point plan for keeping things straight:

1. An easy method for keeping track of titration doses is to use the inexpensive calendar you put in the front of your binder (see page 21).

2. In each day block, write the medication name and correct dose for that day (example: 5 mg at breakfast, 5 mg before bed).

3. Put a check by the medication name when that dose is taken.

4. At the end of the day or the next day, you can jot down a few words about side effects and results, such as "Less appetite. Got all homework done without prompting."

5. This gives you a simple and accurate day-to-day record of how the medicine worked at different levels. At the next appointment, you can show this calendar page to the doctor.

   Various smartphone apps also allow patients to track medication usage. The main thing is to keep it simple and make sure it fits your style.)

Other Easy Tools For Tracking Progress

When your child settles into regular dosages of medications, you'll still need to keep a record of changes over time. Your child's reactions to the medications may change for many different reasons. On the next three pages are logs you can use to:

- List regular medications.
- Record side effects.
- Make simple notes about special behavior episodes that you want to discuss with your team.

Easy Annual Record

You can bring the doctor, nurse or other provider up-to-date by showing these charts at each appointment. Keep all the charts for a year in your binder. Without much effort on your part, the team will have a detailed home record of your child's progress over time.

Read More on Meds
Straight Talk About Psychiatric Medications for Kids by Timothy Willens, MD and Paul G. Hammerness, MD (The Guilford Press, New York, 2016.) helps parents understand what the major medications are and how they work. Important technical terms used by doctors are defined in easy-to-follow boxes scattered throughout the book. Tables and medication logs are printed in the back of this workbook

Medication Log

This chart helps keep information on medicines in one place. Keep an updated version in your binder to bring to appointments and use when talking to doctors by phone. Put a copy inside the medicine cabinet or lockbox to use when you refill weekly pill containers. Make sure the school, each of your child's doctors, and all caregivers have an updated version of this list.

Child's name: _____

Pharmacy name/Ph. #: _____

Last updated: _____

Name of Medication	Total Dosage (Example: 40 mg)	Date Rx started	Date Rx stopped	Directions: How Much/When/Special Instructions (Example: 20 mg tablet morning, 20 mg tablet evening/Take with food/Avoid sun)	Prescription ID Number	Doctor/NP's Name/ Phone Number

Over-the-counter (non- prescription) medicines, vitamins, and herbs (including amounts and when taken):

Special notes for teachers and caregivers (other instructions, side effects to watch for, what to do if side effects are observed):

Medication Side Effects Checklist

Make one checklist for each medication your child takes. (Ask older children to complete this.) Take it along to the next appointment. If any terms on this sheet are unfamiliar, ask your pharmacist or doctor to explain.

Child's name: _____ From Month/Day _____ to _____

Medicine: _____ Dosage: _____

SYMPTOM	YES	NO	OTHER COMMENTS
General Body Functions			
Mouth feels too dry			
Drooling or too much saliva			
Losing weight			
Gaining weight			
Constipation			
Nausea			
Vomiting			
Trouble urinating			
Urinating frequently			
Blurry vision			
Problems with sexual function			
Change in breasts			
Changes in menstrual periods			
Headache			
Lightheadedness, dizziness			
Sleep			
Sleepiness, sleeping a lot			
Trouble getting to sleep or staying asleep			
Muscles and movement			
Feeling restless or jittery, cannot stay still			
Muscles stiff			
Slowness, trouble getting moving			
Shaking or muscle trembling			
Mental function and attitude			
Memory problems, forgetful			
Low energy, easily tired			
Difficult to concentrate			
Too much activity or "pressured" speech			
Irritable			
Anxious			
Thoughts about self-harm			
Any other symptoms			

Behavior Log

Behavior Log for: _____

Medications: _____

Log begun (month, day, and year): _____

Date	What happened, or what was the behavior?	Where and when did the behavior take place? (Example: At school, during recess, while doing homework.)	What was taking place right before the behavior happened? (Example: Change in family plans, child told "no" about something he wanted, argument with sibling.)	Other comments, details, or factors involved? (Meds change? Illness? Event in family?)	What happened AFTER the behavior took place? (What actions did you, the child or youth, or others take?)

Dealing with Treatment Bills and Benefits

4.2: Insurance. When your child or youth has a problem, the goal is simple. You want to find the best help, as quickly as possible, at a price your family can afford. However, in our American healthcare system, the path to that goal is far from simple. A lot depends on your child's or youth's insurance benefits. Benefits are payments made by an insurance company for services your child or youth receives. The rules for getting that treatment can be complicated. That's why you must work with health, behavioral health, and insurance providers to make sure your child or youth gets the benefits he or she needs.

Imagine a giant office building that contains every sort of treatment your child or youth and family can receive. Imagine that inside the different offices of this building are all the organizations that provide treatment, as well as all the providers who work for these organizations. This giant building would have three front doors that might be marked with the following signs:

1. **Door #1:** No insurance or not enough coverage for the treatment your child or youth needs

2. **Door #2:** State-sponsored health insurance

3. **Door #3:** Private insurance through a health exchange or employer

Each door leads to a different series of hallways and other sets of doors that you (and your paperwork) will have to pass through to be able to pay for some type of service.

DOOR #1

No insurance plan or not enough coverage for the treatment your child or youth needs

This means you pay directly for your child's care or get help from free and low-cost services such as the health department (for some services).

Behind Door #1, if your child does not have insurance **coverage**, or your child's plan does not cover a certain type of treatment, or you can't afford to pay your part of the cost, you may be able to use free and low-cost **community resources** such as **prescription drug assistance programs**, county health clinics, or clinics that charge on a **sliding scale** (according to what you can pay). To learn about finding low-cost resources for uninsured families, or how to apply for benefits under Medicaid programs, go to Centers for Medicaid Services, www.cms.gov. Local community programs may be able to help you fill out the forms.

To search for local resources, you can also ***call "211" or go to www.211.org*** and put in your zip code. You can also call your county health department to find out about low-cost resources.

You may need to fill out applications and visit government agencies or community programs to see if your child is eligible for free and low-cost insurance programs that help families who are uninsured, low-income, or have big medical bills. ***In most cases, your child will qualify to get state-sponsored insurance if you can't afford a private policy*** (even if you and other adults in the house are not eligible).

DOOR #2

State-sponsored health or behavioral health insurance plan

This means that a state program pays all or part of the bills for your child's medical and behavioral health treatment.

Behind Door #2, the state pays insurance companies called **Managed Care Organizations** (MCOs) and **Behavioral Health Organizations** (BHOs) to run different types of public health plans. Under this kind of plan, your child gets routine medical care from a **primary care provider** (a doctor or nurse practitioner) who is part of the MCO's network. The BHO has its own network of providers, which are part of a **Community Mental Health Agency** (CMHA) network. That usually means your child gets assigned to a provider–but you can still request someone else if you are not satisfied. Sometimes there is only one MCO for both medical and behavioral health. This is usually called **integrated care**. Look on the back of your child's card.

One way that a child who is on public health insurance can get treatment is through an **Early Intervention Program**. The federal government's name for this program is **Early and Periodic Screening, Diagnostic and Treatment (EPSDT)**, but it may have a different name in your state. A primary care provider (PCP) must **assess** (check) your child for certain health needs and signs of behavioral health problems at an annual medical check-up or at any time you, a teacher, or someone who works with the child notices symptoms. The PCP can refer your child to a **Federally Qualified Health Center**, a local agency, which can evaluate and treat him or her.

DOOR #3

Private-pay insurance through an employer or health insurance exchange

This means that you pay for the plan yourself. Depending on your income, the state may help with part of the cost.

Behind Door #3, if your child is covered by **private pay insurance** benefits, the rules of the behavioral health plan determine where your child can get services. You may need to take your child to a primary care provider to get a **referral** (doctor's order) that allows your child to see a specialist. Sometimes the plan lets you take your child directly to certain behavioral health providers, such as psychiatrists and clinical psychologists who are **in-network** (part of your plan) without getting a referral. Some plans let you choose a provider who is **out-of-network** (not part of your plan) if your child needs a service that is not available elsewhere. Call the number on the back of the card if you are not sure what to do. You can also check your **member's handbook** (written description of your plan benefits). It is usually online; check the card for the plan's website.

Before providing the service, your child's behavioral health professional must contact the BHO to make sure the treatment will be approved. Without this **prior authorization** (permission), you could wind up having to pay the bill yourself. If a specific treatment is **denied** (not approved) by the BHO, you still have options. Sometimes you must call the **customer service** number on your child's insurance card to correct errors in the paperwork or find out whether the BHO needs other **evidence** (facts, such as letters from a doctor) to show the treatment is **medically necessary** (required to treat symptoms). Sometimes you must ask for a **case manager** (an insurance company employee who handles solutions for difficult treatment situations). If that doesn't work, you may need to file an **appeal** (formal request in writing to have the decision changed) according to the rules of your plan.

Call the number on the back of your child or youth's insurance card for help or information.

How to Get Where You Need to Go

Inside this giant "building" full of treatment services, it's very easy to go down the wrong hallway, wander around in circles, or end up staring at a locked door. The rules of your child's insurance plan may be hard to understand and may change over time. Your child's treatment may be denied because the computer has the wrong information or because a small mistake was made in the paperwork. Often, you need to go several places to solve problems or get the right information. That's why you need to use MAPS and GUIDES along the way.

MAPS are different types of written materials (such as a health plan member's handbook or insurance plan website) that explain benefits and procedures or tell you where to go for information.

GUIDES are people who know about different parts of the process, such as customer service associates, case managers, state-sponsored advocates, or the staff in a doctor's office.

The Bottom Line on Healthcare Benefits

Your child may not receive the treatment he or she needs unless you understand the basics of your child's insurance plan and get involved when things get stuck in the system.

A parent often must "pass the ball" between the treatment provider and the insurance provider on a child's team to get services. As you use maps and guides, your job is to:

- Try to get the right medical, behavioral, and developmental health benefits for your child, if he or she doesn't have them now.
- If necessary, look for free and low-cost services that don't require health insurance.
- Learn the basic benefits of your child's plan if he or she is enrolled in one. Send in paperwork on time and do what it takes to keep your child enrolled in the plan.
- Learn the common terms used in this business so you can ask clearly for what your child needs.
- Find out who handles insurance paperwork at the provider's office. Keep a good working relationship with this person. Ask how you can help get benefits approved. Do your part.
- If the insurance plan says "no" to a treatment your child needs, don't quit until the problem is solved.

53

Two Key Words That Open Doors

*Health insurance policies cover behavioral health treatments that are **medically necessary**, a very important term that means the services are required to treat your child's symptoms. When your treatment team's providers want the BHO to approve services that aren't usually covered by the plan, including more days or sessions of treatment, they must show that the services are medically necessary. Sometimes you will have to get experts at the BHO to review your child's case. You may also have to go higher up the chain of command at the insurance company or file an appeal.*

How "Managed Care" Works

When a doctor or other clinician evaluates your child or youth and recommends a treatment plan, you, as the parent, must agree to this plan in advance. If your child receives **benefits** (services that are paid for), the insurance company will also get involved before treatment starts. Providers hired by the company must agree ahead of time that the insurance plan's **guidelines** (rules) do cover those services. This process is called a utilization review, and the providers who do this task (often nurses and social workers) are called **utilization reviewers** or case managers. Sometimes another provider, such as a child psychiatrist, will review your child's case file if there are questions about what your child needs.

You or your child's behavioral health provider can request this added review when trying to change a decision about your child's coverage (services paid for under the plan).

If the recommended treatment fits the plan's guidelines, the reviewer will **authorize** those services (give advance permission for the services and agree to pay for them). In the case of some benefits, such as psychotherapy, the insurance company will often authorize a certain number of sessions. Your child's therapist will have to submit another treatment plan to get more sessions approved.

Sometimes this process takes place with a phone call, but in other cases, written records have to be sent. Either way, **number codes** are used on the paperwork. The codes stand for certain kinds of services and reasons that the services are needed. Sometimes a claim can be denied because somebody accidentally used the wrong code or made a mistake entering the information into the computer. As a parent, you may need to get on the phone with staff in the behavioral health provider's office, or with someone at the insurance company to fix such errors.

A Note about Number Codes: If a claim has been denied, always call customer service first to check if the right number code was used! This can save a lot of time and trouble!

The insurance company that pays for services may do this review on its own, or it may use another MCO. If so, you may need to call one phone number to ask questions about benefits or solve problems, and a different number for questions about billing. When problems occur, you may have to get in touch with that company using the customer service number on the ID card or in the member's handbook (printed or online). You may also need to look for the mental health and substance abuse (MH/SA) number.

1. What's Medically NECESSARY?

Inside that "building" full of insurance services, similar problems may be treated in different ways. For example, a child going through a bad **psychiatric crisis** (behavioral health crisis) may not need to be in a hospital if a program exists to treat those symptoms while the child keeps living at home. The different ways your child can get behavioral health treatment are grouped into a set of categories. Below are the 12 major treatment categories; together, they are called the **continuum of care**.

Continuum of Care

Office or outpatient clinic	Visits are usually 30-60 minutes. The number of visits per month depends on the youngster's needs.
Intensive case management	Specially trained individuals provide psychiatric, financial, legal, and medical services to help the child live successfully at home and in the community.
Home-based treatment services	A team of specially trained staff goes into a home and develops a treatment program to help the child and family.
Family support services	These are services to help families care for their child. Examples are parent trainings or a parent support group.
Day treatment program	An intensive out-patient program (IOP) provides psychiatric treatment with special education. The child usually attends five days per week.
Partial hospitalization (day hospital)	This provides all the treatment services of a psychiatric hospital, but the patients go home each evening.
Emergency/crisis services	These are 24-hours-per-day services for emergencies (for example, a hospital emergency room or mobile crisis team).
Respite care services	A patient stays briefly away from home with specially trained individuals.
Therapeutic group home or community residence	This therapeutic program usually includes 6 to 10 children or adolescents per home; it may be linked with a day treatment program or specialized educational program.
Crisis residence	This setting provides short-term (usually fewer than 15 days) crisis intervention and treatment. Patients receive 24-hours-per-day supervision.

Check Out the Choices

You can find out what treatment programs and services are available in your community by looking at the websites of Community Mental Health Agencies, hospitals, and other health systems in your area. You can call the main number to ask about services and have information sent to you. Your state or local NAMI affiliate may also have this information. Call NAMI's national helpline, 800-950-6264, or visit www.nami.org to find the nearest affiliate. You may also get information from a state chapter of the National Federation of Families for Children's Mental Health. To find one near you, go to www.ffcmh.org

Rules of the Road

Be sure to keep the member's handbook sent by the MCO or BHO. (In some cases, you have to request a handbook by calling the customer service number on your child's ID card or asking a case manager.

Read through the "Benefits Summary" page to get a basic idea of what the plan covers. Highlight information numbers or mark the pages with sticky notes.

Most MCOs and BHOs also have the member's handbook on the company's website. The website address can usually be found on the back of the insurance card.

Residential treatment center	Seriously disturbed patients receive intensive and comprehensive psychiatric treatment in a campuslike setting.
Hospital treatment	Patients receive comprehensive psychiatric treatment in a hospital. Treatment programs should be specifically designed for either children or adolescents. How long your child stays depends on his or her condition and insurance benefits.

Adapted from "Facts for Families: Continuum of Care for Children and Adolescents" fact sheet with permission from the American Academy of Child and Adolescent Psychiatry. For this and other fact sheets, go to www.aacap.org.

2. What's AVAILABLE?

Not all programs and services can be found within every community. These differences will affect the methods of treatment chosen by your child's team. However, if your team can show that services available in another area are medically necessary, it may be possible to use your child's benefits to pay for a service that is not available inside your health system or local area. You may need to get evidence from your child's health provider and other sources to support the view that your child needs to go somewhere else, such as a treatment center or residential program in another city.

3. What's COVERED?

Most health plans have **exclusions**, which are types of treatment that insurance won't pay for under certain conditions. You may have to pay a certain amount per year, called a **deductible**, before the health plan starts to pay. You may also have to pay a small amount, called a **co-payment** or **copay**, for certain visits. Your plan may have an **annual out-of-pocket maximum**, which is the highest amount of deductible and co-payment charges you are expected to pay in one year. An **annual or lifetime maximum benefit** is the most the insurance company will pay for a particular type of treatment over one year or during the whole time your child is covered by that plan.

NOTE: In public health plans, co-payments and annual maximums may be based on your family income. Benefits that are excluded for adults may be covered for children when the treatment is considered medically necessary.

Keep A Phone Log

The best way to get results from **customer service departments** is to keep a log of "who said what and when." This creates a record of your conversations if you need to go up the chain to a higher authority or file an appeal. It also helps you keep track of issues so you can explain the problem to the next person. ("My log shows that during June, I made four calls to customer service about approving in-network benefits for this treatment. On the first call, Andrew told me…but on the next call with Amy, I was told….") Frankly, even mentioning that you are writing this down in your phone log helps to get results.

Finding a Guide with Two Names

Your path to solving problems can be very different depending on whether you have public or private health insurance. If you have public insurance, state law may require that you automatically get assigned to a case manager or have one if you ask for one. In that case, the state has certain agencies you can call with specific problems. The state often pays private advocacy organizations to provide certain kinds of help. Look at the back of your insurance card for information. On the other hand, if you have private-pay benefits, you don't get a case manager unless you have a specific problem. You will usually have to ask for this help, and you may even have to insist on getting it.

Here is a common example of what happens when you call an MCO with a difficult issue:

- Let's say you have a problem getting your private insurance benefits to pay for a treatment from an out-of-network doctor. When you call the helpline number on your child's ID card, you will probably have to go through an automated "menu" of selections.
- Finally, you reach a customer service representative (customer service associate) who will answer with a first name only. ("Hello, this is Andrew, how may I help you?") This BHO employee is trained to look in your child's computer file, answer basic questions, and clear up routine errors.
- Andrew quickly realizes that your problem falls outside those basic guidelines. He puts you on hold with recorded music and finds a supervisor.
- The supervisor tells Andrew–and Andrew tells you–that your provider needs to send in a letter with three pieces of information (we'll call them Info A, B, and C). Andrew makes notes about this solution in your child's computer file. "If you have any other problems," Andrew says cheerfully, "just call the main number and any representative can help you. It's all in the file."
- If you're lucky, that's the end of it.
- If you're not lucky, you must call back again and go through the same automated system in order to reach a human voice.
- This time the call is taken by a different person–let's call her Amy–who needs to hear the whole story again. She looks in your child's computer file to see what Andrew noted last time.

EZ Phone Log Tips

You can keep this log in an ordinary spiral notebook. Just be sure to include the date (month, day, and year) and time of the call.

1. Name of the person and his or her job title.

2. Person's badge or ID # (they should tell you this if you ask).

Manage INFORMATION

Flexible Plans

*Ask about **flexible benefits** if you have private pay
insurance. That means your
BHO agrees that money
targeted for one benefit can
be used to pay for another
level of care. For example,
if your policy allows 30 days
per year of inpatient hospital
treatment, the BHO might
agree to use that money to
pay for 60 days of residential
substance abuse treatment if
you, a doctor or clinician has
provided evidence that this
was medically necessary to
treat your child's or youth's
symptoms.*

- Amy tells you Andrew was quite mistaken, because the rules clearly ask for Info D, E, and F. Just to be sure, Amy talks to her supervisor while you listen to more music.
- Eventually, Amy and her supervisor they decide—guess what?--the provider should have sent info A and Info D in the first place.
- You call your provider's office to report this. It turns out the office manager sent Info A and Info D two weeks ago, but nothing happened. So, you call the customer service number and it all begins again....

When the issue is complicated, you won't get far by dealing with a "first-name-only" phone person. BHOs have special **case managers**, often called **care managers**, who handle these situations. (Even better are **field care managers**, who are assigned to your local community and understand the regional resources in your area. A care manager tends to have more power to get things done and will usually give you BOTH his or her first and last names, plus a direct number. This person can be a huge help in breaking through barriers and finding what you need!

Still, the path can be long and complicated. One insurance company executive recommends that when the customer service associate says, "Just call the main number," you should ask to speak to somebody local. If that doesn't work, ask for a supervisor who can explain the decision. If you still don't understand, ask to talk to that person's supervisor," the executive suggests. Be persistent. If you have an issue with the person on the phone, ask for that person's company ID number. Put this number in your phone log.

"You need to find someone in the organization who can help you identify the issues and get to solutions," the insurance executive urges. "As a parent, you need to keep asking, 'What are our rights? What are our options?' Keep pushing to get the services you feel your child needs."

Guiding Star Point Five: Find SUPPORT

Coping with Crisis

Few experiences are as frightening for a parent as watching a child lose the ability to function in everyday life. Sometimes you can see the clues that a crisis is building. It might be the return of symptoms from a medical condition. It might be a sharp increase in angry explosions, signs of substance (drug or alcohol) abuse, or self-injuries that a child tries to hide. Yet suddenly, you may face an emergency that seems to come from nowhere. Even a strong parent who has weathered many storms can feel numb with shock, filled with rage, or helpless to meet this new challenge. A terrible thing is happening to your family. If you are worn down by a long period of living with your child's symptoms, you may feel an overwhelming wish to let somebody else take over. Yet now more than ever, your child or youth and family will need you to stay strong. Here are some things families who have "been there" think you should know:

1. **This crisis will pass.** It may sound totally obvious—but remembering this truth can be a lifeline when things fall apart at your house. Like any event, crisis has a beginning, a middle, and an end. Life may look somewhat different when it's over, but you and your family will get through the experience and go on.

2. **The team needs you to be a full, equal partner.** In a crisis, providers who don't know your child or youth will join the team. These people have never seen your child look happy and don't know anything about "The Big Picture." The action speeds up and members of the team may miss details that only you can see. You will need to ask good questions and "pass the ball" so that everyone gets the right information. Sometimes we feel like "It's all going wrong, so I must be doing it all wrong." Not true. As long as you keep working with the team, you are your child's or youth's best **advocate**.

3. **You can't do it alone.** Feelings of guilt, shame, or anger about the crisis can prevent a family from reaching out to others. Sometimes people who are close to your family may not always understand what you're going through. Still, part of your job in this crisis is to find useful ways for relatives, friends, your faith community, or others to support you. Don't shut people out.

4. **What you learn from this experience can help you head off the next crisis or handle it more quickly.** By paying attention to how the situation began, ran its course, and was resolved, you can learn the signs of a developing crisis and create a strategy to deal with the next one.

Crisis Language
A **psychiatric crisis** *is a situation in which someone has a sudden, serious change in behavior, with overwhelming emotions and thoughts that don't make sense to others; the person plans or attempts to do something that will cause serious physical harm to self or others. Look back at Guiding Star Point Two for signs that mean your child or youth may be at risk of suicide or violence. If your child or youth seems to be in immediate danger of serious self-injury or violence toward someone else, your FIRST call should be to a youth Specialized Crisis Services number.*

Find SUPPORT

Family Safety Plan

Siblings and other family members may be at risk if your child shows signs of violence. Case managers can often help you form a plan to protect family members from harm in a crisis situation.

A safety plan includes making the whole family aware of how to:

- *Recognize triggers and early warning signs. (These are events that indicate the first stages of an emergency.)*
- *Lower the tension. Recognize the worst-case scenario and do assigned tasks.*
- *Recognize the resolution. (Know when the crisis is over.)*

The Power of Planning

Families who live with repeated crisis often develop a crisis "survival kit" to use in the event a child or youth needs emergency care. The basic supplies in this kit are four kinds of information:

1. Your child's or youth's current records,
2. Emergency resources,
3. A list of questions to ask if your child or youth needs urgent care, and
4. A family safety plan.

If this information is already organized in your binder, you can react more quickly when a crisis begins. What you put in your kit will depend on the unique condition of your child or youth, as well as your family environment. Below are some specific suggestions in the event of a behavioral health (psychiatric) crisis.

Important Records: Emergency personnel will need to know about any past clinical evaluations, medical conditions, and medications your child takes. You may also have to fill out forms with this information if your child is admitted to a hospital or other treatment facility. Make sure your child's Health History and Medications Log are up to date, so you can transfer information easily or show it to staff. In some cases, the staff may let you attach these summaries directly rather than taking down the information all over again.

Emergency Resources for a Behavioral Health Crisis

If possible, you should call the doctor or **nurse practitioner** (**NP**) who handles your child's behavioral health needs. Your child may not need to go to a psychiatric hospital if there are other choices available. In some cases, your child's doctor or NP may prescribe certain medications to treat **acute** (temporary and severe) symptoms. The state usually provides free **specialized crisis services** for children and adolescents whose symptoms pose a serious risk of harm to themselves or others.

Trained staff will come to the child's location to **assess** (determine by using certain rules or standards) the child's need for emergency services. This service is typically faster and less stressful than calling 911. If police answer a 911 call, officers may need to transport your child to a regular hospital emergency room; they'll then call a specialized crisis services team to determine if your child needs emergency care.

To find out about Specialized Crisis Units, ask a local mental health provider or call the nearest psychiatric or residential treatment facility that accepts children.

Twenty Questions to Ask if a Child Needs Psychiatric, Inpatient, or Residential Treatment

1. How will treatment at this facility help my child's symptoms?

2. What are other options for treating these symptoms? How do the options compare?

3. Will my child be placed in an inpatient unit that is specifically designed to treat children and teens?

4. Will my child be admitted and treated by a child and adolescent psychiatrist?

5. How long is the average stay on this unit? How is this decision made and by whom?

6. Which provider will evaluate my child? What types of tests will be used? Who will explain the evaluation results to me and when?

7. What activities will be part of my child's day? How will my child keep up with schoolwork?

8. Is family counseling part of this program? What will we need to do?

9. What should I pack for my child? Can my child have comfort items, such as a favorite stuffed toy or picture from home?

10. What are the visiting policies? When and how often may I get information about my child between visits? May I talk to my child by phone? If so, during what times of day?

11. What behavior management systems are used to enforce rules? What happens if my child doesn't comply? What consequences are used?

12. Does the staff use restraint methods? Please explain how and when.

13. Are staff members allowed to use medications on an as-needed basis to calm children who are agitated or aggressive?

14. How often will the psychiatrist see my child for medication management?

15. What are the roles of others on the treatment team?

16. How much will treatment cost per day? Does this hospital accept our insurance benefits?

17. What will happen if the insurance company denies coverage and inpatient treatment is still necessary?

18. How will I be involved in my child's hospital treatment, including decisions about medications, discharge, and after-care treatment?

19. Once our child is discharged, what plans will be made for his or her ongoing treatment?

20. Will a case manager be able to help us create a family safety plan?

Violent Behavior in Children and Youth

A pattern means certain kinds of actions that happen over and over. A pattern of violence is not "just a phase" and a child won't "grow out of it" without intervention. Seek help if you see any of these behaviors:

- *Attempts to hurt others,*
- *Threats against others (including siblings),*
- *Vandalism,*
- *Use of weapons,*
- *Cruelty toward animals,*
- *Fire-setting, and*
- *Evidence of frequent thoughts about killing or injuring others.*

5

Find SUPPORT

How We Started Team David

When David was in his mid-teens, a co-worker offered to take him on an outing once a week to earn some extra cash. That precious bit of weekly respite was the start of Team David, which now includes eight people who drop by to help in various ways with social and living skills. They have a monthly calendar, so David knows when to expect them. An easy online bookkeeping system helps us run our twice-monthly payroll, including things like taxes and workman's compensation insurance. His disability benefits pay for most expenses now. When problems come up, we do a lot of group emails, and we also try to do a quarterly meeting.

The Bigger Picture: Family Recovery

Most healthcare systems and health insurance plans are designed around a simple goal. They provide (or pay for) direct treatment to people with illnesses in order to help them get well. Unfortunately, that goal does not always fit the needs of children with behavioral health problems and their families. Providers on a treatment team usually receive payment for providing services to the **affected child**, meaning the child who shows symptoms of a disorder. But the truth is that everybody in the family can be deeply affected by the stress and turmoil a child's symptoms create. Siblings may feel overlooked by their exhausted parents or embarrassed in front of peers by a family that isn't "normal." Parents and relatives may blame each other for the symptoms or argue bitterly about how to handle the child. Harsh words spoken in a crisis can be hard to take back when things settle down. The tension of coping day after day can break up marriages and damage relationships.

Yet many families that struggle with serious behavioral health problems will become stronger, closer, and better able to care for one another. No two stories of family recovery are alike, but a common theme is that each family member was able to get the support he or she needed to find a "new normal." So, part of your job as a parent advocate is to keep one eye on "The Bigger Picture" of how your family can stay as healthy and stable as possible. You may have to keep pushing your team to "think family" when building your child's treatment plan. You may have to look for additional services. More importantly, you will need to make contact with other families, programs, or people in your community that can lift you up when you're down and keep you going when you feel like quitting. Steps to consider:

Pay attention to signs that others in the family, including yourself, may need help. Certain behavioral health problems can often show up in several members of the same family. For example, genetic research has shown that about 25 percent of people with depression have a biological (birth) parent or close relative with depression. A person with one biological parent who has bipolar disorder has a 30 percent chance of showing those symptoms; the chances rise to 70 percent when both biological parents have the disorder. A tendency toward substance abuse can also "run in the family."

The constant demands of dealing with a difficult child can take their toll. Yet, many parents fail to seek treatment for their own symptoms until they reach the crisis stage. Some feel their own needs shouldn't matter. Others may fear losing custody of a child if they admit to feeling out of control. They may worry that health or school providers will not treat them seriously if they share information about their own diagnosis.

Money problems will increase the stress. Sometimes a child doesn't have enough insurance benefits. Sometimes the deductibles for those benefits are too expensive for the family budget.

Parents who ignore their own symptoms are setting themselves up for a disaster that can make all the other fears come true. Your child needs for you to be whole, healthy, and able to function. If coping with every-day life becomes difficult, talk to your doctor or look for behavioral health treatment. Try to schedule a session with your child's therapist to talk about ways to handle the stress of dealing with your child. *If you are in a serious crisis and need to talk to a counselor, call the Suicide Hotline, toll-free 800-273-TALK.*

Siblings of a child with behavioral health problems are also at risk if they carry the same **genetic predisposition** (inherited tendency to develop an illness). In any case, they can feel deep conflicts about loving a brother or sister with a serious disorder and get angry about the unfair demands of the situation. Some children act out to get a parent's attention, while others try to be the "extra-good child" who doesn't cause trouble. Neither response will be healthy in the long run.

Try to include family counseling in your child's treatment plan. Part of that counseling needs to focus on practical strategies for making sure that siblings get their fair share of attention from parents, have a way to talk over their questions or fears, and stay safe during a crisis. Dr. Aureen Pinto Wagner, a clinical psychologist and author who directs the Anxiety Wellness Center, recommends that parents try to schedule 15 to 30 minutes per day of YAMA (you and me alone) time with each child. It can be as simple as a walk down the street or a casual chat while cooking dinner. The important thing is to make it a regular ritual the child can look forward to and count on. Meanwhile, be alert for signs that you should seek help for the sibling(s). Such signs may include a sudden change in sleep habits or appetite, poor concentration, low self-esteem, frequent crying or worrying, difficulty separating from parents, frequent physical problems such as headaches or stomachaches, or loss of interest in activities.

Widen your family's circle of support. Families that bounce back from severe problems usually have a support network that plugs them into a caring community and provides help when needed. Many people want to lend a hand or cooperate with you to find ways you can help each other. Sometimes the trick is figuring out what kinds of help will strengthen your family and matching those needs with the support each person is able to give. For example, a school cafeteria worker may be willing to nudge your child into making better food choices. You might partner with another family to take turns providing respite care. An elderly neighbor might watch out her window to make sure your child gets safely off the bus. The wider your circle, the smaller the burden each person must carry, and the more your child will become an independent part of his or her community.

Get Respite

Sometimes you just need a break. The ARCH National Respite Network is a one-stop source for locating respite services in your area (and potential funding to pay for it).

ARCH includes the National Respite Locator, a service to help caregivers and providers locate respite services in their community.

For more information, go to www.archrespite.org/.

You might also check out weekend programs offered by Easter Seals in your area. To find a local affiliate, go to www.easterseals.com.

Your Family's Circle of Support

This worksheet can help you think about people, groups, and programs that might offer practical or emotional support to your family. A strong circle of support that relies on many sources can keep on growing. Ask providers on your team for ideas. If possible, get your child or children to help you list the people who influence them to do the right thing and provide help they appreciate. Don't forget: Cast a wide net! When many people each do a little bit, the circle is stronger.

People and Organizations	Phone numbers, emails, and/or addresses	Possible ways these people or organizations might help
Relatives:		
Friends:		
Faith Community:		
Sources for paid, volunteer, or cooperative respite care:		
Neighborhood and business community:		
School staff:		
Community programs:		
Social agencies:		
Family advocacy organizations:		
Support groups:		

Guiding Star Close-Up: The Classroom-Treatment Connection

What Your Child Needs to Succeed

Federal education law gives special rights to students with disabilities, including those caused by medical, behavioral health and developmental disorders. Though states (and school systems) may each do things a little differently, some parts of the law are the same for every child located anywhere in the United States. The trouble is that laws tend to come with complicated rules, forests of paperwork, and plenty of room for disagreements. Many parents of a child with special needs feel confused, frustrated, upset, or angry about school services. Some parents think schools simply don't want to provide the assistance that their child needs. Some schools think that parents ask for too much, help too little, or expect too many miracles. Sometimes both sides can be correct.

To create an educational program for a child with special needs, the parents and school have to cooperate with and respect one another.

By learning to be an effective **parent advocate**, you can fight less and get more help for your child. An advocate speaks on behalf of someone else who needs support. An advocate gathers facts, helps to plan a strategy for reaching goals, and works with others to find solutions. Your job as a parent advocate is to:

1. Learn what your child needs to make progress at school.
2. Work with the school team to plan practical goals and the right educational program to meet those goals.
3. Make sure that this plan gets put into action–and help to change it if necessary.
4. Form a good relationship with school staff so that everyone on the team can work for your child's success.

Use Your Guiding Star

Education law and education services can be very confusing. It is easy to feel lost and discouraged at times. That's why successful advocates use all five points on the *Guiding Star*. Let's review:

1. ***Set GOALS.*** Believe in your child's or youth's strengths and make sure everybody on the team keeps those strengths in mind when planning goals for your child or youth. Make sure the team understands what interests your child and motivates him or her to learn and achieve. Remember "The Big Picture" and communicate that Big Picture (often) to the team. You will need to keep asking yourself (and maybe others on the team) "Do the goals written on this piece of paper lead us to the Big Picture? If not, what can we do?" When you go to meetings or talk to school staff, be clear about your concerns. In this chapter, you will find tips about

Ten Ways to Be a Great Advocate for Your Child in the School System

1. *Be willing to get involved.*
2. *Be prepared for school meetings.*
3. *Be careful to get the facts before you sign anything.*
4. *Be firm with the team about setting practical goals that help your child make real progress.*
5. *Be flexible about how to reach those goals.*
6. *Be available when the school needs your help.*
7. *Be alert for problems with the plan.*
8. *Be open to creative solutions.*
9. *Be ready to keep learning.*
10. *Be good to yourself.*

No Time? Build a Read-It-Later File

Too busy right now for classes or long books about special education? Start a file of free materials and "read 'em when you need 'em."
Stick these papers in a file folder, or punch three holes in a large mailing envelope and put it in the back of the binder. With this method, you can pull out something for a quick read as you sit in a doctor's waiting room or get ready for a school meeting. The important thing is to start learning. It will make you feel more comfortable with the process, and you'll have a better idea of where to go for more information when you need it.

communicating those concerns and building strong goals that lead to progress for your child or youth.

2. *Learn SYSTEM BASICS.* Schools and community mental health organizations often give out short, simple fact sheets or brochures that explain how special education works. The outline and chart on the next few pages of this chapter also give you some basic details about how your child or youth qualifies for special education services. It is also important to know how things work in your own school system. Attend meetings of the PTA/PTO (Parent Teacher's Association/Organization). Find out who's who in the school system and make sure they know your name. (For example, get to know the school's office staff. They can be a big help!)

3. *Build RELATIONSHIPS.* In many cases, you will need to deal with the same school personnel over the years. Take time to show people they are appreciated and you are willing to help. If you have the time and ability, volunteer to help in the classroom or with other school activities. Fill out paperwork completely and return it promptly. This chapter contains many tips and tricks for working with people, especially before, during, and after IEP meetings. (A big favorite with many parents in our workshops is "Tricks for Remembering People's Names.")

4. *Manage INFORMATION.* Special Education services involve a huge amount of paperwork. You will need a place to store copies of IEP documents, evaluations from school personnel (and possibly outside specialists), test results, formal documents (such as copies of birth certificates), dated copies of letters (such as requests for evaluations), and meeting notes. Develop a filing system that works for you. For some parents, a binder with subject tabs is the best method. Other parents may want to store some of these documents on an electronic device (although it is usually wise to have "hard" (printed) copies with you for most meetings). Learning how to ask questions about tests results and services is another way of managing information. You'll find more about this under "How to Listen to Information About Test Scores and School Services."

5. *Find SUPPORT.* Your child's or youth's needs will change over time, so it's important to find sources of support and new information. Each state has at least one Parent Center. A Parent Center offers free training sessions that teach parents how to get the right school services for children with disabilities. You can also call or write for help with questions or problems that have to do with school special education services. For information, check out the Technical Assistance Alliance for Parent Centers, www.pacer.org/alliance/ or call 952-838-9000. In some cases, local advocacy groups or agencies have peer volunteers or staff (sometimes called "parent partners" or "family support specialists") who are trained to go with you to IEP meetings.

A Diagnosis is Not Enough

Your child does not get services under **IDEA 2004** just because he or she has been diagnosed with a health disorder. Before the school system provides any special services, it must go through a series of steps to show your child's problem has **educational impact** (sometimes called **impact on educational performance**). This means the problem is the main reason your child is not learning as much on average as other students the same age.

To decide whether this is true, the school is required to gather evidence. A parent or teacher may *feel strongly* that a child needs help, but this is not evidence. **Evidence** is a set of facts that can be observed or measured. If you understand what kinds of evidence the law requires and how that evidence is gathered, there is a much better chance you can help your child get the right services.

Below is a short description of how a child is **certified** (made eligible) for special education services. The chart on the following pages also shows the basic steps a school and the child's parent must take. (Some states use different terms for certain steps. This book offers just a general explanation.) You have a legal right to be involved in every part of this process. It is very important to play your part to make sure your child gets the services he or she needs.

Step One: The school receives a request to evaluate your child.

Let's say your child gets distracted easily and has problems sitting still to do regular activities. You take the child to a psychologist who says the child has ADHD (Attention Deficit Hyperactivity Disorder). This is called a **clinical diagnosis**. But having this diagnosis is not enough to make your child eligible for **special education services**.

A **school evaluation** must show that this problem meets certain **criteria** (standards) under IDEA 2004 rules. This evaluation is also called a **comprehensive assessment** because it usually examines many areas of the child's behavior, abilities, and performance at school. Even if a child has been diagnosed by a health provider, the school system must do its own evaluation. (In some school systems, an outside evaluation will be acceptable, but this is unusual.)

For the process to start, it must be a parent, teacher, other school staff member, or **state child protection agency** who asks for this evaluation IN WRITING. When the school system gets this letter, it must either begin the process of getting an evaluation or turn down the request within a certain period of time. (This is known as a **timeline**.) If your request is denied, you can **appeal** (ask a higher authority to decide this issue) by using procedures called **due process rights**. If you don't understand the written explanation the school provides, school staff are required to try to explain it to you.

But before the school can start an evaluation, a permission form must be signed by you, the parent or guardian. The form explains what areas of the child's functioning (intelligence, emotions, etc.) will be examined and why. The form may list the name and phone number of a school staff member to call for more infor-

Document It

Parent advocates say the best habit you can develop is to always WRITE THINGS DOWN. Write down meeting times, who was present, what happened during the meeting--and even how you felt about what happened. Write down who you spoke to between meetings. Include dates and what people said or promised to do. If you are happy and satisfied with the outcome (what happened), these details can be used to establish what works well. If you are unsatisfied with the outcome, this record can be used as a "paper trail" to show what went wrong, so changes can be made.

**The Classroom –
Treatment Connection**

**Don't Wait Until
Kindergarten!**

Well-meaning friends, relatives, or other people around you, including your child's doctor, may say things such as "Don't worry, the child will grow out of it." Don't wait! If your instinct tells you something is wrong with your child's development, ask for an Early Intervention Services or Child Find Evaluation. To get details about the EPSDT (see right column) program in your area, call your local health department.

mation about the evaluation. If not, contact the principal. You can ask what tests will be used, what they measure, and what you will have to do. You can give this person information from other providers on the team, or you can ask that they be contacted. You will probably be asked to sign **release forms** that allow the school to get information from other sources.

If your child is less than three years old, IDEA 2004 gives parents the right to ask the state **Early Intervention Services** agency for a free evaluation of their child. If your child is eligible, a **service coordinator** will be assigned to your family to work out an **Individualized Family Service Plan**. Your child's doctor or other health provider can also arrange for an evaluation if he or she feels your child has a problem or is **at risk** for (may develop) a problem. (See *"Free Services for Birth to Three"* on page 76.)

Children aged three through five can be evaluated through **Early Childhood Intervention Services** provided by the school system. School staff will examine whether your child is likely to develop problems or delays in learning. If the child qualifies, he or she can get free preschool special education services from the school system. Call the local school system office or school board to find out how to request an evaluation.

If public health insurance covers your child, the federal **Early and Periodic Screening, Diagnosis, and Treatment Program (EPSDT)** can assist you. These evaluations are free. The program may be called by a different name in your state, so talk to your child's primary care provider or check with the county health department. Getting these services early in life can be very important to your child.

Step Two: The school system gathers information about your child.

The school system forms an assessment team to evaluate your child. For a behavioral health issue, the assessment team usually includes a school psychologist. It may also include specialists in speech and language, occupational and physical therapy, academic subjects, or certain disorders, such as autism. The team gathers information using the following:

- Standardized tests, checklists, and a health history.
- Observation of the child doing ordinary activities, such as working in class or playing on the playground. Sometimes this observation may include a home visit.
- Information reported by parents, teachers, and others involved in the child's treatment or daily life.
- Evidence of methods the school has tried to deal with this problem in your child's regular education program and how these efforts worked. This is called **Response to Intervention**.

Step Three: The evaluation must show evidence that your child's symptoms have educational impact.

The school psychologist and others who evaluate your child must make written reports about test results, observations, and other information.

Three **eligibility criteria** (standards for qualifying) must be met for your child to be judged eligible:

1. Your child is making less than expected progress in school. **Expected progress** means how much progress state and federal standards say a child of that age should be making during the school year. In a preschool child, it means there is evidence that the child is not developing some learning skills at the expected rate and is **at risk** for making too little progress when he or she enters school.

2. Your child's problem is a MAIN REASON that he or she is making less than expected progress. If other factors, such as lack of certain academic skills or lack of ability to speak English, are the MAIN causes, a behavioral health issue alone won't qualify your child. These other causes are called **rule-outs**.

3. Your child's problem falls within one of the **13 disability categories** listed under the IDEA 2004 law. Some behavioral problems diagnosed by health providers (such as conduct disorder or oppositional-defiant disorder) are not included under this law, even if they interfere with learning. The evaluation must show that your child's condition fits into one of the categories listed in the sidebar at right.

If all three criteria are met, the child is considered to have a **disability** (also called a **disabling condition**) and has the right to get services under IDEA 2004. The **assessment team** will offer the evidence and make recommendations. However, the actual decision about whether your child is eligible for services is made at a meeting between YOU and staff from the school system. If you DON'T get involved, the school system staff can meet and make these decisions without you. If you DO get involved, the school system must meet with you and get your permission for the next steps. *GO TO THIS MEETING IF YOU POSSIBLY CAN!*

Step Four: A meeting is held to decide whether your child is eligible for special education services.

The parent and a school system representative meet with members of the assessment team and other school staff. If the child is shown to be eligible, then the team writes an **Individualized Education Plan** (**IEP**). That step may happen at the eligibility meeting, or at another meeting if more time is needed.

NOTE: "IEP" is an abbreviation that schools tend to use three different ways. It can be used to mean the meeting itself, the education plan written at the meeting, or the legal document produced in this meeting. The IEP team is the people

IDEA 2004 Special Education Disability Categories

- *Autism*
- *Deaf-blindness*
- *Deafness*
- *Emotional disturbance*
- *Hearing impairment*
- *Intellectual disability (formerly called mental retardation)*
- *Multiple disabilities*
- *Orthopedic impairment*
- *Other health impairment (ADD/ADHD)*
- *Specific learning disability*
- *Speech or language impairment*
- *Traumatic brain injury*
- *Visual impairment*

States or school systems choose whether children ages three through nine may get services for "developmental delay" even if they don't fit one of the categories above.

The Classroom –
Treatment Connection

What's a 504 Plan?

Section 504 of the Rehabilitation Act is a civil rights law that guarantees access to education for children with disabilities. 504 Plan "accommodations and modifications" are changes that assist children with special needs in a regular education program. Some children that don't qualify for special education services under IDEA 2004 will qualify to receive accommodations under Section 504. To get these accommodations and modifications, a school evaluation must show that the condition interferes with the child's ability to learn.

The accommodations and modifications are described in a 504 Plan document signed by the parent and the school system representative.

involved in this meeting, including you as an equal partner with the school.

The eligibility decision has two parts. First, the team decides to **certify** your child in one of the 13 types of disabilities listed under IDEA 2004. Unfortunately, educational law does not use the same categories that health providers do. For example, a child with ADHD is certified under the category "Other health impairment." Mood disorders such as depression are classified as "Emotional disturbance." If a child also has another difficulty, such as a hearing problem, "Multiple disabilities" might be chosen. As a parent, you can give your point of view or present evidence about which category best fits your child's situation.

If you agree with the school system's decision to certify your child in the **disability category** chosen, you sign the first part of the **eligibility report**. The **school system representative** (person legally representing the school system) also signs. Next, the team must decide whether reasonable changes in the regular education program will be enough to help your child make the **expected progress**. If these changes (called **accommodations and modifications**) are enough, the child won't qualify for special education services. However, he or she may be able to get these changes, even if they're not in the IEP Plan, through a **504 Plan** (see "What's a 504 Plan?" at left). To learn more about how this decision is made, see "The Story of Jenny and John."

If you and the school system representative agree that the **regular education program** cannot meet your child's needs, you both sign the second part of the report. At this point, your child is now **eligible** for special education services. However, there are still many decisions to be made (and forms to fill out) to create the **IEP document**. The next part of the process is to decide exactly what kind of special education program your child will receive.

Step Five: The IEP team writes an education program to meet your child's special needs.

This step may occur at the same meeting as the certification decision in Step 4, or it may be saved for a later meeting if the team needs more time. The IEP team writes a plan to help your child make educational progress. By law, all plans must have three basic parts:

1. **Goals** for how much progress your child can be expected to make this year, what the steps toward making this progress will be, and how the progress will be measured.

2. **Services and supports** that will help the child make progress toward the IEP goals. These services might include speech therapy, school-based behavioral counseling, or special equipment.

3. **Placement** in a regular or specialized classroom based on what is needed to deliver those services and supports to achieve the goals.

Some children receive special services in the regular classroom or outside the classroom for part of the day. Others may be placed in special classrooms at the regular school or in special schools with other children who have similar disabilities. In some cases, a teacher comes to teach a child at home for a short period. Sometimes, a child with problems the school can't handle must be placed in another facility.

Here are some things to remember about this important document:

- Signing this form means you give permission for those actions. To make sure you understand what you are signing, the school system is required to explain all parts of the IEP document to you. The school system must also provide a foreign-language or deaf interpreter if you ask for one.

- You do not have to sign the IEP document if you do not agree with the decisions proposed by the school system. If you disagree, you and the school will need to meet again to work out your differences.

- If you still can't agree, the IDEA 2004 law and state procedures offer ways for you to appeal. You can also appeal if the school system does not carry out the plan as promised. However, you and the school system must make every effort to agree on a plan.

- What happens when you don't agree with the school's recommendations may depend on what state you live in. It's a good idea to learn more about education SYSTEM BASICS in your area. Local advocacy groups and your state's Department of Education website may be two good places to start.

- Showing written evidence that you have made a **good-faith effort** (tried to be fair, sincere, and involved) is important in case you ever need to file an appeal to get your child services. This effort will also help to create a good relationship with the school so the plan will work better. (See more about written evidence in "Tips for Writing Letters.")

Step Six: The school system meets with you once a year to review the IEP.

A new IEP must be completed and signed (in most states) one year from the date the old one was signed. At this meeting, the goals and objectives are reviewed to see what progress your child has made.

Goals may be added in, taken out, or changed in some way. Based on the new set of goals, the IEP team considers whether your child's placement or services need to be changed. The IEP team always includes YOU.

Be aware that an IEP can be changed more than once a year. If your child's condition changes or the plan isn't working well, either you or the school can request a meeting to revise the IEP at any time.

Sometimes the parent and school can agree (in writing) to small changes without holding a meeting. However, you can always ask for a meeting if you feel

Who's on the IEP Team?

Many school providers may be needed for your child's IEP meeting. Most often, they include:

- *Principal;*
- *School psychologist;*
- *Classroom teacher (often, this is the home-room teacher if your child is in middle or high school);*
- *Any specialists that have tested your child or who have special knowledge about the issues;*
- *Special education teacher;*
- *Supervisor, in some cases;*
- *Someone from a special classroom or school if the school system is proposing such a placement for your child;*
- *You, and*
- *The child, beginning at age 16, or younger when necessary.*

You Don't Have to Go It Alone

Some parents may feel uncomfortable facing an IEP meeting room filled with school staff members. If you are one of those parents, plan to bring someone with you. It doesn't have to be an expert. You can bring a relative or friend who takes notes or observes what goes on at the meeting.
You are also entitled to bring:

- *Your child's other parent, even if he or she does not share custody;*
- *Other providers on the treatment team or outside experts who know about the issues;*
- *Someone from an advocacy organization to give you advice and support.*

If you plan to bring others, let the school know, ahead of time, who will attend. Courtesy is important in building a good relationship for the long haul!

one is needed. In any case, though, the school evaluation that started this process must be updated once every three years. You don't need to make another request for this evaluation.

For summertime, sometimes a separate plan is written to provide a summer program called an **Extended School Year Program** (**ESY**) so that your child can keep up the progress he or she has made. If you think your child may "lose" academic progress during the summer break, be sure to ask about Extended School Year (ESY) programs before Thanksgiving if possible. Ask how children qualify for the program, as well as when and how the school "measures retention." Depending on the program's rules, it may be necessary to test your child after winter break.

The Story of Jenny and John

Here is an example of two cases in which the same clinical diagnosis might lead to similar kids' getting different services in school. Imagine two children named Jenny and John. Each one has been diagnosed with major depression. At this point, medications and therapy work well for Jenny. The former "A" student has become a "B-minus" student this year, but her annual test scores show that she is making enough progress in a regular education program to keep up with state standards.

To help her progress, Jenny needs some modifications in the usual classroom routine. For example, she needs to be able to leave the classroom for a mid-morning snack because the medications she is taking make her very hungry and less able to concentrate. The teacher has also created a quiet place in one corner of the room where Jenny can go if she's having a bad day. Unless something changes for the worse, Jenny's depression may not be considered a disabling condition that makes her eligible for a special education certification. However, the modifications in her regular education program (the snacks and the quiet place) are written into a **504 Plan** document, which is signed by her parents and the school system.

John, on the other hand, is falling behind. He missed a lot of school days last year because medications and therapy have not been able to control his depression. Test scores show he has not made enough progress to keep up with other students his age. The teacher reports that John can't work on projects with other students. The school evaluation has ruled out other causes for this lack of progress. John's depression appears to have educational impact. If the regular education program can't be modified to meet his needs, the IEP team may recommend that John be certified to receive special education services.

 NOTE: In some states, IEPs are now signed electronically. If so, you may never have to put a pen to paper. Also, it may be possible to "attend" a meeting by phone conference if you can't be there in person.

Review: How Your Child Gets Special Education Services

The Basics:

- A federal law called the Individuals with Disabilities Education Improvement Act (IDEA 2004) guarantees that a student with disabilities will receive a "**free appropriate public education**" (**FAPE**) that is "designed to meet his or her unique needs."
- When the evidence shows that your child's needs cannot be met in the regular education program, he or she is entitled to an individualized program of special education services.

TO GET THESE SERVICES, THE PARENT AND SCHOOL MUST (ORDINARILY) GO THROUGH THE STEPS BELOW. This is a general explanation of the process. Regulations (and what things are called) can be different from state to state, so it's important to start learning how the system works where YOU live. Fact sheets and workshops produced by advocacy groups can be a big help. Your state's department of education website may have useful information, too.

STEP 1 *The school receives a request to evaluate your child. That starts a timeline (number of days by which the school must act or respond).*	**Your child has symptoms:** 1. physical 2. behavioral 3. developmental
	Your child's school will have to carry out a school evaluation for your child to be certified to receive special education services. A request for a school evaluation is made in writing by: • you (the parent) OR • your child's teacher OR • other school staff OR • a state child protection agency
	If the school AGREES, you must sign a form giving permission to evaluate your child. The **Parent Consent form** includes: • areas to be tested • why these areas are being tested / If the school DOESN'T AGREE, you may appeal this decision to a state agency, using **due process rights**. The school must explain these rights to you.

STEP 2 *The school system gathers information about your child's condition, abilities, and school performance.*	A school **assessment team** is formed to evaluate your child. The team usually includes the school psychologist and may include other school specialists, depending on the child's problems.
	The team gathers information using: • Standardized tests, checklists, and health history • Observation of the child • Information reported by you, the teachers, and others involved in your child's education or treatment • Evidence about methods the school used to handle the problem in the regular program (**Response to Intervention**).

| **STEP 3** *The evaluation must show evidence that your child's symptoms have educational impact.* | The assessment team makes a written report that includes:
• Test results
• Information gathered or observed, and
• Recommendations about whether your child is eligible for services. |
| | For your child to be eligible, the evidence must show that his or her disability meets three eligibility criteria (standards):
• Your child is making **less than expected progress** in school than the state expects for a child the same age (or your child is **at risk** of not making this progress, if preschool age).
• The disability is the main reason (sometimes called the "significant reason") your child is not making the expected progress. The evidence must **rule out** other causes, such as lack of ability to speak English.
Your child's problem **fits the criteria** for one of the disability categories under federal law. |

STEP 4 *A team meets to decide whether your child is eligible for special education services.*	The decision to certify your child for services is made at an **eligibility meeting**. Most people actually call this an *Individualized Education Program* (*IEP*) meeting, because once the child is eligible, the people in the meeting become the *IEP Team* to create this program.
	The *IEP team* includes: • A school system representative, other school staff, or experts in certain disabilities. • YOU, as an equal partner with the school. • Someone you can invite to go with you to offer information or support. • The school principal, classroom teacher, or homeroom teacher. • Members of the assessment team who will be able to report test results, observations, and recommendations.
	If the evidence shows your child meets the criteria, he or she will be **certified** (declared eligible) in one of the *federal disability categories*. The disability categories are not the same as those used in a clinical diagnosis.

If you and the school system representative AGREE to have your child certified under a certain category, you both sign the IEP eligibility form.	If you DON'T AGREE, you don't sign. You and the school system try to work out differences.	If you CAN'T AGREE, you can appeal to a state agency, using your due process rights.

If reasonable changes in the regular program can help your child make enough progress, your child will not be eligible for special education under the IDEA 2004 law.

"IEP" is often used in conversation to mean (1) the child's special program; (2) the written document that describes the program; and (3) the meeting to create the document.

STEP 4 *continued*	However, even if your child isn't deemed eligible for special education services, he or she may still get certain services in the regular classroom under Section 504 of the federal Rehabilitation Act. This is called a **504 Plan**.

STEP 5 *The IEP Team writes an educational program to meet your child's special needs.*	Writing the program to help your child may occur at the IEP meeting to certify your child or at a later meeting.
	When writing the program, the IEP team makes decisions about: • **Goals** for the kinds of progress your child should make in different areas of educational need by the end of the year. This includes the specific steps for making this progress, as well as how and when the progress will be measured; • **Related services and supports** that can help your child reach the goals, or • **Placement** in a regular or special classroom, special school
	The decisions made by the IEP team are written into a set of forms called the **IEP document**.

If you and the school system representative AGREE to the decisions, you both sign this set of forms.	If you DON'T AGREE, you don't sign the forms. You and the school system try to work out differences.	If you CAN'T AGREE, you can appeal to a state agency using due process rights.

When you and the school system reach an agreement, the forms are signed (by hand or in some systems electronically) and the child can begin receiving special education services on the date written in the IEP document.

In some states, services may start even if a parent doesn't sign by a certain date. In other cases, a parent may sign off on the parts they agree on (so services can get started) and set a date for a new meeting to revisit the parts on which they don't agree.

STEP 6 *The school system meets with you at least once a year to revise the IEP.*	A new IEP must be written every year. This is called an **annual review**. The IEP team reviews how the goals were met. Goals may be taken out, added, or changed. Based on the new set of goals, the team will review whether your child needs any changes in placement or services. At every IEP meeting, you have the right to show new evidence, state your concerns, suggest ideas, and ask questions.
	An IEP can be changed more than once a year if conditions change or if the plan isn't working well. Either the parent or school may request a meeting to **modify** (change) the IEP.
	The school evaluation must be updated at least every three years.

THE BOTTOM LINE ON THE IEP

BE THERE
And
BE AWARE

You have a right to attend the IEP meeting. Be there if you possibly can.
- The school must tell you the time and date of the meeting at least ten days in advance. The school must try to find a date and time when you can be there. Sometimes you can even meet by phone or videoconference.
- If you can't be there, the school needs to keep you informed of the results by phone, email, or mail.

You have a right to have all parts of the IEP explained to you.
- The school system is required to use a set of printed forms. The forms have many pages and technical terms. The staff must explain all the details in words you can understand.
- Don't sign anything if you don't understand or don't agree.
- Don't be embarrassed to keep asking if something doesn't make sense. You may see a flaw that nobody else has noticed.
- Don't feel rushed because the meeting is taking a long time or people in the meeting need to leave. The school system must keep meeting with you until the whole job is done.

An IEP meeting is just the beginning.
- After the meeting, a parent needs to stay involved. Set up a regular way to communicate with your child's teacher.
- If your child is having a really tough time, or if parts of the plan do not seem to be working, meet with the teacher and other school staff to brainstorm ideas.
- Even if you don't have much time, let the school know you are willing to help solve problems with your child's program.

Free Services for Birth to Three

From birth until age three, children qualify for **Early Intervention Services** if they have a developmental delay, or a specific health condition that will probably lead to a delay. This includes genetic disorders, such as birth defects or hearing loss, as well as difficulties with speech or movement. The state usually pays a local non-profit organization to provide these services to families free of charge. A healthcare provider may identify signs of possible delays at the hospital where a child is born. Primary care doctors or nurse practitioners conduct simple tests during regular check-ups to look for some of these important "milestones" of development. The parent or a childcare provider might also notice the child is not developing as quickly as others of the same age. If you have a concern about your child's development, call 211, or go to 211.org to find an Early Intervention Services provider in your area. Services are usually provided in a setting such as your home or a childcare center.

A few months before your child's third birthday, you and the Early Intervention team will discuss the transition out of Early Intervention Services. The service coordinator will set up a planning meeting. This will help you prepare your child for the next stage of education. Some children will no longer need services. If the child is eligible for preschool special education, a member of the local school district will work with you to plan this transition.

(Credit: Kathy Bentley, Kathy's Parenting Solutions)

What to Do Before the Meeting

Getting prepared for an IEP meeting is very important, but it doesn't have to be difficult or stressful. Below are some areas to consider:

- **Get a date that works for you.** At least 10 days in advance, the school system must send a notice with the date, the time, and the place where the meeting will be held. You can **waive** (agree not to claim) this right if it is more convenient for you and the school. There should be a name and phone number on the form. If not, call the principal to get the name and number of a person you can contact about the meeting. If you can't be there, call the person named on the form right away to schedule a new date and time. The school must try to plan the meeting at a date and time you can attend. If you (or someone such as a parent sharing custody) cannot be there, ask the school to set up a conference call.

- **You don't have to wait for the school to set the date.** Send an email or drop off a note at school with dates and times that are convenient for you (as well as dates that you cannot be there). Be sure to date this letter. When it comes to IEP meetings, it is always better to "do it in writing and get it in writing." (See more on "Tips for Writing Letters," page 87).

- **Find out what the meeting will cover and how long it will last.** The purpose of the meeting should be listed on the notice. If you aren't sure, call and ask what will happen in this meeting. Once the meeting date is set, find out how much time is scheduled for the meeting. If you are told "30 minutes" and you have five issues to discuss, that won't be enough time. Ask for more time or a different day.

- **Let the school know what you need, and what you want to discuss.** Surprises are not a good thing at an IEP meeting. Just as the school should tell you what to expect, you should tell the school what you want. This shows courtesy and good faith. It also lets others prepare, which means less wasted time at the meeting. Your consideration encourages the school to show you the same courtesy and respect.

- **Let the school know who will come to the meeting.** This is courteous and helps staff plan for enough seating space and copies of materials. If you feel it is necessary to record the meeting, notify the school because school officials will want to do the same. Ask for any special services you need, such as an interpreter. You may write this request in your own language; the school is required to get it translated.

- **Look at your child's school records beforehand.** The law gives you the right to see your child's permanent record (usually known as a cumulative record or CR) if you make a request in writing. You are granted this right by

Go to the Source

The source most often quoted in books and websites about special education is Wrightslaw, the website and book series produced by attorney Pete Wright and psychotherapist Pam Wright. Browse through http://www.wrightslaw.com for almost anything you need to know about your child's educational rights. You will also find detailed advice about working effectively with the school system.

The Wrights' handbook, "From Emotions to Advocacy: The Special Education Survival Guide" (Harbor House Law Press, Inc., Hartfield, VA, 2006), is well-organized and easy to skim as you get ready for the IEP meeting. Also included are sample letters and helpful worksheets for keeping records.

Take Care of Your Documents

NEVER write on original documents except very lightly in pencil. Don't use a marker or highlighter pen. You may need to copy those documents to send to others when making a request or appeal. NEVER send your original documents to anyone. Keep them in your binder or files. If someone at an IEP meeting wants to copy one of your original documents, DO NOT LEAVE IT BEHIND. Get it back in your binder before you walk out the door.

IDEA 2004 and the **Family Education Rights and Privacy Act (FERPA)**. You should ask to look at the entire CR, as well as any other school system files that have information about your child. However, the school has the right to charge you to make copies of these files. The CR of a child with problems tends to have a lot of pages. Many parents prefer to go to the school or school system office, look through the file, and copy only the material they need for the issues at hand. (Others feel it is necessary to have a copy of everything. Do what seems right to you. It is always possible to change your strategy later.)

- *Get copies of important documents, which could include:*
  - Any past tests or evaluations you don't already have.
  - Any past IEP forms you don't have.
  - Letters sent between you and the school, if you don't have copies.
  - Any letters, reports, or notes by school staff about your child's behavior or performance.

- *Prepare your list of concerns and questions.* For a shortcut, look back at the "My Child's Strengths and Needs" list on page 9. Which of these apply to your child's behavior and performance in school (or attitude toward school)? Put those at the top of your list of concerns. Look through your child's file and list any questions that occur to you.

- *Add any questions about the evaluation process or test results you have already reviewed.* NOW, go back and try to narrow down the list to five or six items. Think about wording. Focus on the result, not the service. Rather than listing an item as "Getting Tommy a classroom aide," you may want to list "How can we make sure that Tommy finishes assignments without needing the teacher's constant attention?"

Prepare your "Meeting Toolkit."

Plan to bring your binder to the meeting because you may want to refer to documents. Some parents like to put sticky notes on the edges of the reports or documents they are most likely to need. If you need to pull out a document to show it to others at the meeting or if someone needs to copy something, make sure to get your original document back. Don't forget to take your list of concerns.

Other items to bring:

- Notepad or notebook paper. Some parents like to take notes on paper inside the binder. Others like to use an inexpensive, three-hole-punched notebook.
- Writing materials, including two pens, a pencil, highlighter, and sticky notes if possible.
- A picture of your child. Many IEP meetings include experts or school officials who have never met your child. Passing around a picture helps the meeting focus on a child, not a "case."
- Any documents you have sent the school or the school has sent you that relate to this meeting. You may need to show that you made certain requests or

sent information on a certain date. Having a dated document to pull out will prevent lost time and arguments. If these documents are filed in your binder, mark them with sticky notes on the edges so you can find them when needed.

- Other support materials. Bring any outside evaluations or letters about your child's disability, even if you have already given a copy to the school.

- Food and drink. IEP meetings can sometimes go on for hours, and you will not be at your best when you are hungry and thirsty. As a friendly gesture, some parents like to bring snack foods or cookies to share. At least make sure that you have water or your favorite beverage to keep you going.

What to Expect During the Meeting

The IEP meeting may have a written **agenda** that is passed out to everyone at the table. If you don't get one, politely ask the facilitator (that is, the person who runs the meeting) to list the main points that will be covered. Write them down. You will need to look at them as the meeting goes on. A typical IEP meeting usually begins in this way:

Statement of purpose: At the start, a **facilitator** will usually state the purpose of the meeting, saying for example, "We're here today to determine Mary's progress in reading." If this is not the purpose stated in the notice you received, ask why.

Introductions: Next, everyone present should be introduced by name and job title. Again, if this doesn't happen at the start of the meeting, ask for it. (See "Tricks for Remembering Who's Who," page 81.

A summary of your child's **Present Level of Performance:** This means the results of your child's evaluation(s) and other comments from the people in the room. This information will be summarized in the IEP document and used to build your child's educational program.

Prepare Your Head

Look back at "Practicing Assertiveness" on page 43 for tips on looking and acting like a "parent partner." If you are nervous about speaking up in a meeting, write down a list of points you want to make and practice saying them in a strong, direct way. Ask a family member or friend to listen to your points and look over your list of concerns. The more familiar you are with special education terms, the more confident you will feel. Flip through your information file or go to some of the special education websites listed in this chapter. If you are in touch with others through an advocacy organization or support group, call your contact person for a last-minute boost of confidence.

**The Classroom –
Treatment Connection**

Get a Head Start

If possible, meet with the school psychologist, reading specialist, or other evaluators ahead of time to review test results. You will feel less pressured, and it will give you a chance to get better prepared for the IEP meeting. If you forget to ask about something (or the information fades out of your brain by the next day), write down those questions to bring to the IEP meeting. Give the school advanced notice that you want to meet with an evaluator to review test scores. Some parents include this request when giving permission for the evaluation by attaching a note or writing the request directly on the bottom of the form. As with anything you sign, KEEP A COPY.

Skip the Drama: How to Listen to Test Scores

It can be very painful to sit there trying to look calm and collected while other people give you bad news about your child. However, it is really important to understand this information. The evidence contained in all those strange-sounding words will be used to establish your child's eligibility for services. It will also be used to determine what types of services your child will receive. Here's what often happens and what you can do to get a grip.

The scene: A crowded IEP meeting full of school staff. When the meeting started, you were introduced to five new people. You have already forgotten at least three names.

The action: A school psychologist pulls out several sheets of paper covered with numbers and graphs. Words such as "percentile rank" and "processing speed" begin to fill the air.

Your inner response: TMI (Too Much Information)! CUT (Can't Understand This)! Help!!

Your outer response: "Oh...umm...yes...I see... right."
Instead, you could say:

- "Sorry, this seems very confusing. Could you run that by me again...?"
- "I'm not really a math person. Are you saying...?"
- "What does this mean in terms of my child's ability to...?"
- "Can you explain why...?"
- "Do you think these results are true reflections of my child's performance in...?"
- "So, if you had to sum up this set of results in one sentence..."

TAKE YOUR TIME. Don't feel rushed because others in the room seem impatient or start having side conversations. Test scores confuse many parents. School specialists are not always good at explaining complicated matters in simple terms. You can help them practice this important skill! Most school personnel want you to understand what test scores mean so you can understand their recommendations.

See the IEP in 3D

Many parents think that IEP teams meet to discuss and "vote" on a child's program. Not true: An IEP team tries to reach consensus (general agreement) on issues, but does not actually make the final decision. The various teachers and experts are present to offer information, write goals, make recommendations, and brainstorm ideas. All final decisions are made by two votes. The parent gets one vote. The other goes to the system representative, also known as the **Local Education Agency (LEA) representative**. This person (called by other terms in various systems) is assigned to represent the school system during the meeting.

The person's signature on the IEP form will **obligate** (require) the system to take the actions described on those forms. Your signature as a parent means you give **consent** (legal permission) for the school to take those actions. When–and only when–both of you sign, it's a deal. Everyone else signs the forms to show they attended the meeting, and may check a box to show their agreement or disagreement with the decisions made.

Why is this important? Because an effective parent advocate sees a meeting in "3-D vision." A 3-D approach means you Deal Directly with the Decision Maker. Here's how to do it: Listen carefully (with an alert, interested expression) to every person's comments.

HOWEVER, when you want to make an important point or request (as in, "I feel that..." or "Would it be possible to...?"), talk directly to the one person in that room who has the most power to say "yes" to what you want. In an IEP meeting, the system representative has the power to agree or disagree with your requests.

The system representative is often, but not always, the highest-ranking person in the room. That may be the school principal or the special education supervisor. If you are not sure, politely ask before the meeting begins, "Who will be serving as the system representative today?" (This indicates your knowledge of the system!)

Before the meeting starts, make sure your seat at the table allows a clear view of this person. If not, say, "Could we shift around? I want to be sure I can see everyone. That spot would be best for me, I think."

Sometimes the system representative will have to duck in and out of the meeting to take phone calls or deal with problems elsewhere. If that happens, try to restate important questions or requests again when that person returns ("Mrs. Blank, while you were out, I mentioned that... How do you feel about this?"). If that doesn't seem possible, make a note to bring up your point when the goals are being written ("Mrs. Blank, earlier when you were out, I mentioned and I believe we never resolved....").

Why "3-D Vision" works: When you give the decision maker your attention, you don't waste time trying to talk others into changing their opinions. You put the decision maker in the position of speaking for the whole group. That person is more likely to listen directly to what you say and to tell you clearly what the school system is willing to do.

Tricks for Remembering Who's Who

The IEP team will often include several people whom you have never met. Some of these people may be school specialists who evaluated your child. Others may be experts brought in to give advice or school officials from higher up in the chain of command. Introductions are usually made at the start of the meeting, but it's hard to absorb this information when so much is happening. You may feel embarrassed to ask people's names again.

There are three good reasons to keep a firm grasp on knowing who's who: First, it is more courteous and professional to address people by name. Second,

The Real Report is the FINAL Draft

The results of an evaluation may be in "draft" (unfinished) form at this meeting or at the IEP meeting. In some cases, that happens because the evaluator wants you to look over the report for anything that is incorrect or has been left out. Ask the psychologist or other school specialist when a final copy will be ready. Request that it be mailed to you or left at the school for you to pick up. When it comes, file this report in your binder under the "School" section. If it doesn't arrive, ask again. If you see any errors in this copy, write a note to the principal asking to have the errors corrected and a new copy sent to you. Keep all the versions, but (lightly, in pencil) mark the last one "Final" at the top of the first page.

you need to know which person is the speech pathologist, which one is the resource teacher, and so on, in order to understand the information each person is presenting. Third, you may need to contact some of these people later.

At the beginning of the meeting, try one of these methods for connecting names and faces.

Business Card Bingo: Ask each member of their team to give you his or her business card. Ask anyone who doesn't have a card to write the name and job title on a small piece of paper. Lay these cards out in front of you in the same pattern that people are seated at the table. Glance down at the cards when you need to jog your memory.

Seating Chart: Draw the table's shape on a piece of notebook paper. Outside the "table," make a circle for each person at the meeting. Pass the paper around, starting at one corner of the room, and ask each member of the team to print his or her name and job title in or near the circle that goes with that position at the table. Then put this paper in front of you so you can glance at it when needed.

Ask someone at the table to help you organize the cards or start the seating chart. Getting others involved can be a great icebreaker, because almost everybody has trouble remembering names. Also, it will help save time and let you give full attention to the meeting. Put a star next to the person who is acting as **Local Education Agency or school system representative** as a reminder to keep your focus on him or her. After the meeting, write the date on this paper and file it with your meeting notes in the "School" section. Keep all business cards!

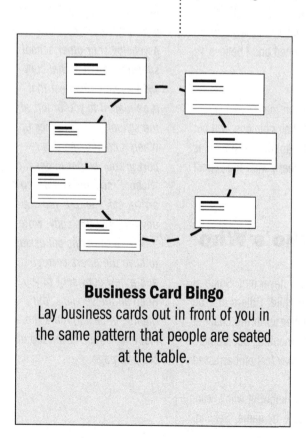

Business Card Bingo
Lay business cards out in front of you in the same pattern that people are seated at the table.

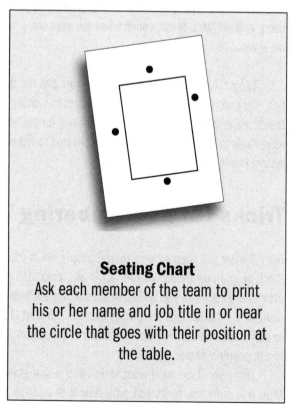

Seating Chart
Ask each member of the team to print his or her name and job title in or near the circle that goes with their position at the table.

Building Goals That Really Work

Some parents walk into an IEP meeting thinking, "My child needs..." a certain type of classroom or service (such as speech therapy, a personal aide, or a certain teaching method). Sometimes those parents are right about the service, but wrong about how the IEP process arrives at those decisions. This may cause a lot of conflict. In the IEP process, all decisions about your child's program begin with **Annual IEP Goals**. These goals are written into the IEP document, along with a series of details about how your child should make progress toward the goals. Based on what is needed to meet those goals, your child is placed in a certain kind of classroom and receives certain types of services.

Just as a house needs to be built on a strong foundation, the IEP needs to be built on strong goals. Weak goals are general statements of what a child should know or become. There is no clear way to show if the goal has been reached. Strong goals identify specific, practical skills and specific methods for producing evidence that your child has learned that skill.

Many parents feel totally lost when the team starts writing IEP goals. The IEP forms contain many codes, percentages, abbreviations and tiny check-off boxes with terms such as "Criteria for Mastery." Don't panic. You aren't picking up a hammer and nails to build this house by yourself. You are working with the builder (your school district personnel) to make sure this house has all the right parts. if you know what the main parts are, you can ask the right questions.

How Goals Are Built

Your child's evaluation (together with other input at the IEP meeting) is summarized on a part of the IEP document called **present level of performance**. It identifies your child's **areas of need**, which means the broad categories of skills in which your child needs to make progress. Areas of need might relate to academic areas (for example, "Math Reasoning") or how a child gets along with others and deals with emotions (a "Social/Emotional" area).

For each area of need, the IEP team writes an annual goal that sums up the overall progress it is hoped your child will make in the coming year. Underneath this annual goal will be a description of the specific skills the child will learn, along with how and when those skills will be measured. These details are usually called **objectives** or **data points** because they describe ways that school staff will be able to tell whether your child has learned that skill.

Guide for the Journey

The Complete IEP Guide: How to Advocate for Your Special Needs Child (NOLO, Berkeley, California, 2014) by attorney Lawrence M. Siegel provides a detailed blueprint for developing your child's educational plan. Laws are explained in plain language. Tear-out forms in the back of this book offer terrific fill-in-the-blank letters, information logs, and worksheets, such as an "IEP Material Organizer" sheet and a checklist for when you visit your child's class.

Making a Powerful Point

A mother, whose son with autism was attending a new school, created a short PowerPoint to show school staff what he and the family visualized as a perfect day after he exited from school at age 22. The staff loved it--and it set a goal to work toward.

The Four Building Blocks of a Strong Goal

Let's say a child named James has an area of need called "Written Expression." This category includes skills such as handwriting, spelling, and learning to organize ideas. At the top of the goal sheet, the IEP team writes a broad annual goal they want James to reach by the end of the year. This might be, "James will achieve functional writing skills at the fifth-grade level."

One of the objectives under this goal is to improve James's spelling skills. To build a strong overall goal, this objective should contain four strong building blocks called CONDITION, BEHAVIOR, ACCURACY, and RELIABILITY.

Let's say that one of the objectives under James's goal is to improve his spelling. Here's how the building blocks will show up:

CONDITION: This means how or when James will do something to show he has learned the skill.

Example: "When prompted by staff no more than three times to get his materials ready and begin work, James will…."

BEHAVIOR: This means what the child is expected to do.
Example: "…complete a fifth-grade level spelling test…."

ACCURACY: This means how well the child must do this task.
Example: "…with 80 percent accuracy…." (that is, James will spell eight out of ten words on the test right).

RELIABILITY: This means how often the child must do this behavior accurately to show "mastery" (prove the goal has been met).

Example: "…in three out of five trials." (This means, for example, that on a weekly spelling test, James will get the target score on a spelling test at least three weeks out of every five weeks he takes a test.)

Strong goals have three important qualities. A strong goal is:

1. CONCRETE. The goal describes exactly what sorts of tasks the child has to do in order to learn that skill. "James will work cooperatively and independently with others" is not as strong as "James will work in a small team of at least two other students to complete a project without direct support from staff."

2. MEASURABLE. The goal tells how information will be gathered about whether the goal was reached. "Teacher observation" is not as strong as "With staff help, James will be able to describe at least four ways he contributed to the team's work."

3. TIME-LIMITED. The staff knows when and how often the task must be measured. For example: "By the end of the first nine-week grading period, James will complete at least two team projects with other students."

Do Your Child's IEP Goals Pass the Building Blocks Test?

This worksheet can help you do a quick "building inspection" on your child's goals. It can be used at least four ways:

- **USE IT FOR EACH GOAL.** During an IEP meeting, ask a school staff member to help you fit the parts of the goal under each building block. You can use one blank sheet for every goal. Some building blocks may be written on the IEP form using codes and numbers. Ask the team to explain it in simple words. If one building block is not filled in or you don't understand the words used, this goal may need more work. NOTE: This exercise can encourage team members to slow down and explain technical terms.
- **USE IT AS A WARM-UP.** You can use this sheet during an IEP meeting for the first one or two goals as a way to help the team "learn" how to explain goals to you. This reminds everyone that you will insist on strong goals that include these building blocks. The discussion will tend to shift in that direction.
- **USE IT AS A REFERENCE.** You can keep this sheet in front of you as a reminder of the building blocks and as a way to make notes about questions to ask.
- **USE IT AS AN EXERCISE.** You can do this exercise on your own, using the goals on your child's old IEP or another child's IEP. The more you practice, the easier it will be to spot the strengths and weaknesses of an IEP goal.

Area of Need (Example: Written Expression): _____

Annual Goal (Example: "James will gain functional writing skills at the fifth-grade level"): _____
_____

CONDITION: This means how or when the child will do something. (Example: "When prompted by staff no more than three times to get his materials ready and begin work, James will....")
_____
_____

BEHAVIOR: This means what the child is expected to do. (Example: "...complete a fifth-grade level spelling test....")
_____
_____

ACCURACY: This means how well the child is expected to do it. (Example: "...spelled with 80 percent accuracy," means eight out of ten words will be spelled right.) _____
_____

RELIABILITY: This means how often the child must do it accurately to meet the goal. (Example: "...in three out of five trials," means James will spell enough words right at least three times for every five tests.) _____
_____

FINAL INSPECTION: Is this goal:
- ☐ **Concrete?** Does it describe exactly what sorts of tasks the child has to do in order to learn that skill?
- ☐ **Measurable?** Does it tell how information will be gathered about whether the goal was reached?
- ☐ **Time-limited?** Do the staff members know when and how often the task must be measured?

The Classroom – Treatment Connection

Follow Up

Although an IEP form is long and complicated, many small details of the plan may not be written down. By writing a short thank-you note to the school system representative, you put those details on record and make sure busy staff remember to do as they promised. For example, the letter might say:

Dear Mrs. Blank,
Thank you for a productive meeting to create my daughter Anna Castillo's IEP. It is my understanding that the school psychologist, Dr. Jose Padillo, will call me within two weeks to review Anna's reading test scores, which were not available yesterday. If this is not your understanding, please contact me at the phone number or email address listed above. I look forward to working with you.
Sincerely,
Maria Cortez (Mother)

Before You Leave the Meeting

Review all decisions. The person in the room who is recording decisions should read everything back to the team. Listen very carefully and interrupt politely if anything is incorrect or has been left out. Feel free to do this as many times as necessary. If something went by too quickly, ask the person to read it again or show it to you.

Sum up any matters that are not written into the IEP or have been left for next time. ("OK, my understanding is that we've decided to…and our next steps will be…") Make sure it is clear WHAT will happen, WHO is responsible for those next steps, and WHEN they will happen. It's a good idea to request that these details be written into the meeting notes, which become part of the IEP document. Ask whom you should contact if you have any further questions about the IEP document later on.

Remember to:
1. Take copies of all documents you signed.
2. Put all the documents and materials you brought with you to the meeting back in your binder.
3. Thank everyone for taking part in your child's meeting.

What to Do After the Meeting

Give yourself credit for doing your job as a parent advocate. Many parents forget this important step. You deserve a pat on the back for trying to find your way through a difficult process.

File all documents back in your binder as soon as possible. Go back to your notes and fill in any details while your memory is still fresh. If someone took notes for you, fill in any extra things you remember.

Put any important meeting dates or deadlines on the calendar in the front of your binder or other location. For example, if the school psychologist promised to send you a corrected copy of the psycho-educational evaluation report in a week, mark that date on your calendar as a reminder to call if you don't get it. If the IEP team needs to meet again to finish working on goals, pencil in a reminder to check back in a week if you haven't received notice of a meeting date.

Reread the IEP document carefully. Make sure you understand the contents, and if not, call the "contact" staff person with questions.

Send a short thank-you note to the system representative. If the school principal did not fill this role at the meeting, send him or her a copy of the letter (See the sidebar at left for a good model letter).

Tips for Writing Letters

Attorney Pete Wright, co-author of many educational advocacy books and the website www.wrightslaw.com, says, "If it was not written down, it was not said. If it was not written down, it did not happen." He means that you need to be able to prove by written evidence that things happened the way you say they did.

Many people don't like to write letters or feel they don't know how to do it well. However, a letter can be very simple and still do the job. Great letters can be a big help, but "good enough" letters are better than phone calls or casual talk. It's okay to use a form letter, such as the samples you find in many guides and special education websites. It is usually better to type a letter, but a neatly handwritten note can be fine for sending everyday information, like a message to a teacher.

Here are a few important reasons for writing letters rather than simply talking to school staff, social services agencies, etc.:

- A statement in writing (on paper or by email) is a permanent record.
- You can think out exactly what you want to say and double-check for errors.
- If you are upset, you can wait to "cool off" before you reply to another person's words or requests.
- A letter makes it less likely that people will misunderstand, ignore, or forget what you want.
- In a letter, you can state (for the record) a reasonable time for getting a response to your request. (Example: "I look forward to getting your response within ten days.")
- In many cases, the law requires school district personnel to respond or act within a certain time (the **timeline**) after getting your letter. Your letter or signature on a form may begin a timeline for getting your rights or your child's rights.

For better results, a letter should be addressed to a specific person. Call the school or agency to ask for the right name and be sure to spell it correctly! Add the person's title or office for the record. (Example: Mary Jones, Principal, Happy Valley Primary School.)

Sources: Support and Training for Exceptional Parents, STEP Record Keeping information Packet, www.wrightslaw.com, Tennessee voices for Children (www.tnvoices.org).

Reminders for Letter-Writers

A letter is a record of what happened. It must be written so that someone who was not part of the events (like a special education supervisor or hearing judge) can understand clearly what happened.

When you write a letter:
1. Use your child's name in the letter.
2. Use your full name.
3. Add who you are if your last name is different from your child's. For example: Mary Green (mother).
4. Date the letter.
5. Include your address and phone number.
6. Sign the letter.

NOTE: Always keep copies of all emails and letters you send to school district personnel. Put these in your binder.

**The Classroom –
Treatment Connection**

IEP for Real Life

During the last four years of David's school career, we began to make lists of what he would need to live independently. It was a little overwhelming to discover how many skills a person needs just to get through a day! Yet it helped the IEP team to focus on setting goals that would really make a difference. We began to notice small details, such as David's difficulty writing an email or leaving a message on voice mail. He needed to learn how to handle his wallet safely at a check-out counter. Those things started showing up on his IEP. Focusing on practical skills made a huge difference in his independence and self-confidence.

Transition Planning with Your Teen

Transition is a term used in education law to mean a period of years between the late teens and early 20s, when a young person's task is to gain the skills needed for independent living. This passage is never smooth or easy, but it can be especially tough for people with special needs. A youth who has spent years struggling to cope with medical, developmental or behavioral symptoms will often grow up more slowly than others the same age. He or she may have more trouble getting used to new situations, making safe choices, or handling responsibility. Events that often mark a teen's first steps into adulthood–a summer job, a driver's license, leaving home for college–may not happen in the same way. The young person may follow a different path with a different schedule and may require many helping hands along the way.

The parents of a teen with these conditions are also in transition. The clock is ticking, and they may feel helpless to provide what the youth needs to survive in the world. One mother worries, "Will my son never be able to do what a boss tells him without getting into a rage?" Another wonders, "How can my daughter go to college, when she still needs me to get her out of bed in the morning?"

Meanwhile, the teen, like most teens, probably resists being told what to do. Parents in transition have the tricky, often thankless task of holding on while letting go. School is one place this will happen. At age 16, or sooner when necessary, a youth in special education becomes part of the IEP team, with the right to have a say in what kinds of training and services he or she receives. ***Your job as a parent in transition is to help your youth learn to be a full working member of this team, planning for things to come.***

Back to "The Big Picture"

People often ask a youth, "What do you want to BE when you grow up?" A more useful question for a teen in transition might be, "How do I picture my everyday life when I'm an adult?" That picture will have several important pieces: a satisfying job (and whatever study it takes to get the job); a place to live; activities to fill free time; transportation; and a community that includes friends, loved ones, and people to give support when needed.

IDEA 2004 requires the school system to develop a transition plan that describes the path your youth intends to take after high school. It must include the training and services that will help prepare your youth for that path. However, the transition planning process can end up being little more than long, empty words on paper unless YOU and your youth keep everyone's eyes on "The Big Picture." At every IEP meeting, keep asking, "How does this education program get from here to there by the end of high school?"

Big-Picture Planning

One way to start creating "The Big Picture" of life after high school is to look back at the strengths, concerns, and dreams that you and your youth listed on page 9. On another sheet of paper, start filling in some more details. You and your youth may choose to work on this "future story" together or separately. Think: What would an average weekday include? What kind of work setting might fit the youth's strengths and personality? (Quiet and routine? Active, with lots of variety and people nearby? Indoors or outdoors?) Does he or she want to live at home after high school? If not, how much supervision or security might be needed? What about transportation? What about free time? Who are the people in the youth's life who already give help and support? Who else and what else will need to become part of the youth's life in the next few years?

NOTE: Many teens can only take this process in small doses.

Thinking about the future can provoke a lot of anxiety, as well as push-pull feelings about the parent's role. ("Take care of me, but get out of my life!") You may want to keep your own plan in the background at first, using it as your youth's source of ideas as you, your youth, and the rest of the team start to create the transition plan.

The Basic IDEA for Transition

Under IDEA 2004, the IEP document that is in effect when a youth turns 16 must contain statements covering four main elements:

- Your youth's intended path after leaving high school. This statement will describe the youth's work, education, and other life plans after high school. This might include a job, college, vocational school, or a training program.
- Your youth's transition needs as they affect the education program. This means the IEP team must indicate what kinds of classes, training, or other experiences are necessary to meet your youth's needs to prepare for this path while in high school. NOTE: This may also include services to help your youth explore different work or study choices.
- Necessary transition services. The IEP must list services that the school system will provide to help your youth develop the skills necessary to make his or her plan a reality. In addition to academic study or training programs, these services might include special coaching for skills your youth will need. Some examples might be learning how to write a resume or learning to use public transportation.
- Non-educational agencies. The IEP must state whether agencies in charge of certain benefits, health programs, or job training can provide services, and how to get help from those services. The plan will also describe how the school will get involved in working with those agencies.

Transition Means More Than Work and Study

The statement about a young adult's path after high school should also contain a brief description of the plan for:

- *the youth's intended form of housing,*
- *transportation,*
- *how the youth will keep safe and healthy,*
- *who will take care of his or her daily needs, and*
- *how the youth will be involved in the community.*

As the youth gets older, this picture needs to become more detailed. The more that picture of the future comes into focus, the more your team can develop services and supports to help your youth live independently.

How to Stay in Touch with Your Child's or Youth's Teacher(s)

At the start of the IEP period, talk to the teacher about the best ways to stay in touch. The method must fit the child's or youth's age, wishes, and ability to communicate on his or her own. These are two common choices:

- *Communications journal: The parent and teacher write messages to each other in a notebook that the child or youth carries back and forth to school each day.*
- *Daily/Weekly Communications Sheet: Many teachers make up a form with symbols or check-off boxes to report behavior and with room to write comments. At the bottom, the parent writes a response, signs it, and sends it back.*

Ten Things Teachers Want You to Know

1. Most teachers aren't experts in education law. A classroom teacher may not always understand your child's rights under IDEA 2004 or be aware of all the services your child can receive. Start by assuming they want to help, then help them figure out how to do it.

2. Teachers work for the school system. Like any other employees, they must follow the school rules and carry out the decisions of their superiors.

3. Teachers want your child to learn and be successful. Sometimes a teacher may not understand what your child needs. Ask if the teacher would like an article or fact sheet that describes your child's disability or offers classroom ideas.

4. Teachers want you to be involved. They need you to help them understand your child's behavior. They need you to participate in carrying out behavior plans and solving problems. Show up for school meetings and volunteer to help, even in small ways.

5. You will get better attention by respecting the teacher's time. Find out how and when the teacher likes to be contacted. Schedule meetings in advance and show up on time. If possible, let the teacher know what the issues are ahead of time so he or she can be prepared.

6. Like everybody, teachers can be nervous about change. A teacher may resist a new method because he or she can't see how it fits into the routine. Encourage your IEP team to include any necessary teacher training in your child's plan. IDEA 2004 permits this service.

7. Teachers want to hear from you before a small problem becomes a big problem. Often, a problem can be easy to fix. Send a note or an email. Be polite. Assume the teacher doesn't want trouble and would rather keep parents happy.

8. Teachers make mistakes. However, they don't appreciate being embarrassed in front of their bosses. Be tactful. Talk to the teacher first before going to a higher-up.

9. Teachers like to be kept up to date. Let them know about medication changes and events at home that might affect behavior at school.

10. Teachers like to be praised for their efforts. Write thank-you notes often. Send holiday cards. Tell the principal or supervisor about the teacher's good work.

Glossary

A

Accommodations and modifications. Changes made in a regular education program to help a child or youth make educational progress. Certain criteria must be met to be eligible for these changes (see 504 Plan).

Acute. Symptoms that are both temporary and severe.

Affected child. A child who shows symptoms of a behavioral health or other disorder.

Agenda. A document, which lists the main points to be covered in an IEP meeting.

Annual (IEP) goal. An educational goal that the school system expects your child or youth to reach by the end of a year, as part of his or her Individualized Education Program (IEP).

Annual IEP review. A meeting to review a child's IEP and make any necessary changes in goals, services, or placement within the next year.

Annual or lifetime maximum benefit. The maximum amount that your healthcare plan will pay for treatment of a particular kind of health problem, either per year (annually) or during the entire time your plan is in effect.

Annual out-of-pocket maximum. The maximum amount that you will be required to pay per year for certain types of treatment under the terms of your health insurance plan.

Appeal. A formal request for a decision to be changed by a higher authority.

Areas of need. Broad categories in which your child needs to improve in order to make progress in school, as determined by the IEP team and included in the IEP document.

Assess. To evaluate a person's medical, behavioral, or educational condition in order to determine what services the person needs.

Assessment team. A team of school staff or consultants assigned by the school to evaluate a child. For behavioral health issues, the team usually includes a psychologist and may include specialists in certain disorders.

At-risk. In possible danger, especially for developing a problem.

Authorize, authorization, pre-authorization, prior authorization. Approval given by the insurance company for a treatment that is shown to be medically necessary and covered by the person's health care benefits.

B

Behavioral Health Organization (BHO). An insurance company that manages benefit plans for mental (behavioral) health or substance (drug and alcohol) abuse treatment.

Benefits. Also called "coverage." The contract between an insurance provider and the insured person that obligates the insurance company to pay for certain medical or behavioral health treatments.

Black-box warning. A Food and Drug Administration (FDA) warning that alerts doctors to a possibly serious side effect or complication that might be caused by giving a medication under certain conditions.

C

Care manager. A type of case manager for a health insurance plan whose job it is to help people find options for getting treatment approved or to solve unusual problems with the benefits plan.

Case manager. A staff member in a medical, behavioral health, education or insurance setting, whose job is to set up services, coordinate services, or help solve problems for a client.

Certified or certification. Eligible (allowed) to receive special education services. A child has to be certified under one of the IDEA 2004 law's 13 disability categories in order to receive special education services.

Claim. A request to get a certain service or treatment paid by the insurance company.

Clinical diagnosis. A health provider's description of a problem, made after an evaluation is performed.

Clinician. A provider who evaluates your child (usually a clinical psychologist or licensed clinical social worker); may also provide therapy.

Community Mental Health Agency (CMHA). A large mental health center that has a contract to provide services to people who are enrolled in public health insurance plans; sometimes called a Community Mental Health Organization (CMHO). A CMHA is located in each county.

Community resources. Agencies, organizations, and programs that provide services for people with different types of needs.

Comorbid diagnosis. An additional or "secondary" diagnosis, when a person meets the criteria for more than one disorder.

Comprehensive assessment. See "School evaluation."

Confidential Information. Information about a patient that a health provider cannot tell police, employers, or others not involved in the person's treatment, except under certain conditions.

Consent. Legal permission.

Continuum of care. The span of care options available for behavioral health patients, ranging from a short office visit to inpatient hospital treatment.

Co-payment or Copay. An amount you must pay when you visit a healthcare provider. Varies according to health plan.

Coverage. Also called "benefits." The contract between an insurance company and the insured person, promising to pay for certain treatments under certain conditions.

Criteria (one criterion, many criteria). Standards that must be met in order to be included in a certain category, usually for the purpose of qualifying to receive certain services.

Cumulative Record (CR). A child's permanent school record.

Customer Services (or member services) representative. An insurance company employee who answers routine questions or solves problem by phone.

D

Deductible. The amount of money you must pay out-of-pocket before your insurance plan will begin to pay for certain types of services.

Denied. Not approved for paid coverage of services under a particular health plan.

Diagnosis. The overall term that health providers use to describe a problem. A behavioral health diagnosis is reached after an evaluation that may include conversations with you, your child or youth, and others, as well as tests, examinations, or laboratory studies.

Disability, Disabling condition, or 13 disability categories. A condition that interferes with a child or youth's ability to learn or function at the same level as others of the same age. To view a list of the 13 disability categories outlined under IDEA 2004, see page 69.

Disorders. Physical changes, thoughts, feelings, or behaviors that cause problems with activities and daily living.

Drug interactions. Possible problems that may occur when one drug is used at the same time as another drug.

Diagnostic and Statistical Manual of Mental Disorders (DSM). A publication of the American Psychiatric Association that lists and describes behavioral health disorders. Healthcare providers use the DSM categories to diagnose illnesses.

Due process rights. Procedures that must be followed in order to appeal a decision made by an organization, such as the school system or a mental health center.

E

Early and Periodic Screening, Diagnosis, and Treatment Program (EPSDT). A public health insurance program aimed at finding, diagnosing, and treating problems in children and youth.

Early Childhood Intervention Services. Services available through the school system for children ages three through five who have medical, behavioral, or developmental problems, or are at risk of developing problems.

Early Intervention Services. Services to help children from birth to age three who have medical, behavioral, or developmental problems, or are at risk for developing problems.

Educational impact. The effect of a disability on how a child makes progress in school compared to others of the same age.

Eligible or Eligibility criteria. To qualify for services or treatment, usually defined by meeting certain conditions or standards.

Eligibility meeting. A meeting to determine whether a child is eligible to receive special education services. This meeting always includes the parent, if he or she is willing and able to be involved.

Eligibility report. A report that determines whether or not a child or youth is qualified to receive special educa-

tion services because a regular education program cannot meet educational needs.

Evaluation. The process of examining a person's condition or behavior in order to find out the problem. An evaluation can include conversations with you, your child, and others; a physical examination; other tests; and laboratory studies.

Evidence. A set of facts that can be observed and measured.

Exclusions. Types of treatment that an insurance plan will not pay for under certain conditions.

Expected Progress. How much educational or developmental progress that state expects a child or youth of a certain age to make under typical circumstances.

Extended School Year Program (ESY). An IEP developed for the summer months in order to help a child keep up with the progress he or she has made during the school year.

F

Facilitator. A person who runs or directs a meeting.

Family advocacy organization. An organization that provides information, training, or support to families and works to influence the public, legislators, or government agencies on their behalf.

Family Education Rights and Privacy Act (FERPA). A federal law regulating how a child's or youth's school records can be used.

Free Appropriate Public Education (FAPE). Your child's right, under the federal IDEA 2004 law, to an education "designed to meet his or her unique needs." Guarantees the right to special educational services when the regular education program cannot meet a child's needs because of a disability.

Federally Qualified Health Center. A local health center that can assess and treat patients.

Field care manager. A special case manager employed by a Managed Care Organization or Behavioral Health Organization who is based in the local community.

504 Plan. An educational plan that lists accommodations and modifications that will help a child who meets certain criteria to make progress in a regular education program. Some children or youth with behavioral health disorders who do not qualify for special education services under the IDEA 2004 law will qualify for 504 plan accommodations.

Flexible benefits. An agreement by the insurance company that money targeted to pay for one type of health plan benefit (for example, in-patient hospital treatment) can be used to pay for another level of care (such as residential treatment).

G

Genetic predisposition. A tendency to develop an illness that is inherited through one or both biological parents. A predisposition means a person may develop that illness, and so should be watched carefully for symptoms.

Genetic traits. Physical and mental qualities or conditions a person inherits from a biological ("blood") relative.

Good-faith effort. A legal term that means the person or agency has shown a sincere effort to be fair, honest, and willing to solve problems.

Grievance. A formal written complaint to a higher authority about a problem with a provider.

Guidelines. Rules set up to determine the conditions under which certain treatment services will be approved for payment by an insurance plan.

H

Health history. A form that contains basic information about a person's medical history. This will usually include physical diseases, behavioral health issues, medications, allergies, immunizations, family health history, and developmental history.

Health Insurance Portability and Accountability Act (HIPAA). Federal law requiring healthcare providers, under certain conditions, to get permission before releasing patient information.

I

Individuals with Disabilities Education Improvement Act of 2004 (IDEA 2004). A federal law that guarantees the right to educational services for students with disabilities aged three through 21 (or through the end of the school year in which an eligible student turns 22).

Individualized Education Program (IEP). A program of educational services for a student with a disability. In the school system, this term is often used to refer to 1) a meeting to certify a child or youth for special education services; 2) the education plan written at this meeting; and 3) the legal document that describes the program.

IEP document. A legal agreement, signed by the school system representative and parent(s), that describes goals, services, and placement to be provided for a child or youth with a disability.

Impact on educational performance. See "Educational impact."

Individualized Family Service Plan. A plan developed by a social agency to provide services to a child or family.

In-network provider. A member of a group of healthcare providers whom a patient is allowed to use under the terms of a health insurance plan.

Intake interview or appointment. The first appointment with a new health provider or social agency. At an intake interview, you give information and discuss symptoms.

Integrated care. A treatment approach in which providers work together to give the best care for a patient.

Inpatient psychiatric unit. A special unit in a hospital where patients with severe behavioral health problems stay 24 hours per day while receiving treatment.

L

Local Education Agency (LEA) representative. The school official at an IEP meeting who has the power to make the final agreement between you and the school system about your child's educational program.

M

Managed Care Organization (MCO). An insurance company that the state pays to run a public medical health insurance plan.

Medically necessary. Treatments that are necessary in order for a patient to be appropriately treated for his or her symptoms.

Member's handbook. A handbook that sums up the benefits that an insurance plan provides, as well as contact information, such as providers' phone numbers and information numbers. Also available on the company's website, in most cases.

Mental Health/Substance Abuse (MHSA) telephone number. A phone number (listed in the handbook and on the health insurance ID card) that a person must call to get help with questions or problems relating to behavioral health insurance benefits.

Mood Disorders. Disorders that affect a person's ability to regulate emotions. Examples: Depression, Bipolar Disorder.

N

Number codes. A combination of numbers used by medical and insurance systems to represent patient diagnoses and services provided.

Nurse Practitioner (NP). A registered nurse (RN) who has done further advanced training in patient care. An NP can provide many of the same services as a doctor, including ordering tests and prescribing medicine. An NP with special training in psychiatric disorders may be called a Licensed Psychiatric Nurse Practitioner.

O

Objectives (also known as data points). In an IEP, specific steps that describe what a child must learn or accomplish in order to master a stated goal.

Obligate. Require. If the school system representative signs an agreement with you, the school is legally obligated to do what it says it will do.

Off-label. A drug prescribed for a condition or a type of patient it was not originally intended to treat. This means that the United States Food and Drug Administration (FDA) has not yet approved a drug for a certain use in a certain patient group. The doctor may prescribe it anyway, based on his or her own experience and the experience of other doctors and researchers.

Out-of-network. A provider who is not on the list of a certain insurance company's contracted providers.

Over-the-counter-medication. A medication that can be sold without a prescription from a doctor.

P

Parent advocate. A parent who is involved, aware, and active in the management of his or her child's care and who speaks up for the child's best interests.

Patient portal. An electronic system used by healthcare providers to maintain records and exchange information with patients and caregivers.

Pediatrician. A doctor who specializes in children's overall healthcare.

Permission to Release Information. See "Release Form."

Prescription Drug Assistance Programs. Programs to help buy medications for people with low income.

Present level of performance. A portion of the IEP document that describes your child's or youth's current ability to function and make educational progress in school.

Primary care doctor. Sometimes known as a family doctor, family practice doctor, or primary care provider; a doctor who sees patients for general healthcare needs. A pediatrician or family physician may serve as a child's or youth's primary care doctor.

Prior Authorization. See "Authorization."

Private pay insurance plan. A health insurance plan that you pay for yourself or that you get through an employer.

Provider. An individual or organization that provides medical or behavioral health services.

Psychiatric crisis. A situation in which a person has a sudden, severe change in behavior that creates a serious risk of harm to that person or someone else.

Psychiatric medications. Drugs prescribed by a doctor or nurse practitioner (NP) to treat behavioral health problems.

Psychiatrist. A medical doctor (MD) who has done several years of extra training in diseases and disorders of the mind. A psychiatrist can prescribe medicines.

R

Referral. A primary care provider's order that will allow your child to see a specialist under the terms of your health insurance plan.

Regular education program. A typical educational program designed for children or youth of a particular age group.

Release form (also called "Permission to Release Information"). A form that you sign giving permission for one health or educational provider to share information with another provider or organization.

Residential treatment center. A facility where a person receives behavioral health or substance abuse treatment 24 hours per day.

Respite services. A worker or organization that provides temporary care for a person with an illness so regular caregivers, such as parents or other family members, can have a break.

Response to Intervention (RTI). Evidence of methods a school has tried in order to deal with a child's problem in the regular classroom.

Right to privacy. A patient's right, under certain conditions, to keep personal information private and not share with others.

Rule-out. A condition that would disqualify a child or youth from being certified as having a disability under IDEA 2004. For example, if the main reason for a child's or youth's lack of progress is poor attendance at school, a behavioral health issue alone would not be enough to qualify that child or youth to receive special educational services.

S

School evaluation (also called a "comprehensive assessment"). An evaluation performed by the school system; this evaluation examines many areas of a child's behavior, abilities, and school performance.

Service Coordinator. If a child or youth is eligible for early intervention services because of a medical, behavioral, or developmental problem, a person called a service coordinator is assigned to help the family create a plan for getting treatment and other services.

Sliding scale. A system in which people are charged fees according to what they can afford to pay.

Special education. Services and methods used to educate students with disabilities who qualify under the federal IDEA 2004 law.

Specialized Crisis Services. A unit of trained staff that comes to a child's location to assess his or her need for emergency care.

Standardized assessment tools. Tests commonly used to evaluate behavioral health or educational problems. Some typical standard assessment tools include cognitive and adaptive tests, psychological evaluations, developmental evaluations, and educational evaluations.

State child protection agency. A government agency responsible for evaluating and protecting the physical, emotional, and mental well being of children and youth.

Symptoms. Signs of disease that may include physical changes, thoughts, feelings, and behaviors.

System representative. See "LEA representative."

T

Test battery. A series of tests to help determine your child's needs.

Timeline. The time frame within which a person or organization must respond to the action taken by another person or organization.

Titration. The process of increasing a person's medication dosage from a small amount of a drug to a larger dose over a period of days or weeks.

Therapeutic dose. The amount of a drug or medicine that is effective for the patient.

Therapist. A person licensed by the state to give treatment for physical, behavioral health, and/or developmental disorders.

Transition. A term used in education law to mean a period of years between the late teens and early twenties, when a young person's task is to gain the skills needed for independent living.

Trauma. A serious, negative event in a person's life that can affect behavior, emotions, and physical health. Examples: Sexual abuse, family violence, death of a close relative, or involvement in a natural disaster.

Treatment plan. A medical plan that lists treatment steps, which can help a child or youth reach goals created by providers and parents or guardians.

U

Utilization review, Utilization reviewer. The process by which insurance companies decide whether certain health services are covered by a person's health insurance plan. The reviewers, often nurses or social workers, are employed by the company.

OTHER NATIONAL RESOURCES

Anxiety Disorders Association of America
www.adaa.org
Describes anxiety disorders, treatments, and common co-occurring issues. The website also offers specific information for teens and young adults. You can download the free brochure "Got Anxiety?" for college students.

Autism Society of America
www.autism-society.org
Facts about autism and latest treatment options; ASA chapters listed by state.

The Balanced Mind Parent Network
www.dbsalliance.org
An excellent source of recent findings about depression and bipolar disorder; the site includes resources for older children, teens and young adults, mood charts, online support groups, and databases of local support groups.

Children and Adults with Attention Deficit/Hyperactivity Disorder (CHADD)
www.chadd.org
www.help4adhd.org
Database of local chapters and support groups; facts about ADHD in children and adults.

Jason Foundation
www.jasonfoundation.com
Provides education and training for students and families on prevention of suicide. Also includes toll-free help line 800-SUICIDE for youth in crisis.

Juvenile Bipolar Research Foundation
www.jbrf.org
Among the offerings on this site are brief screening tools that help families know when to seek help.

OASIS@MAPP
www.aspergersyndrome.org
The Online Asperger Syndrome Information and Support (OASIS) Center has joined with MAAP Services for Autism and Asperger Syndrome to create a single resource for families, individuals, and medical professionals who deal with the challenges of autism.

NAMI (National Alliance on Mental Illness)
www.nami.org
800-950-6264
NAMI is the nation's largest grassroots mental health organization, with affiliates in every state and more than 1100 communities. NAMI is dedicated to improving the lives of persons with mental illness, their families, and their communities through programs that offer education, support, and public advocacy.

International OCD Foundation
www.iocdf.org
Facts about Obsessive Compulsive Disorder.

National Tourette Syndrome Association
www.tourette.org
Information for adults, teens, and children about Tourette Syndrome.

National Federation of Families for Children's Mental Health
www.ffcmh.org
The National Federation of Families for Children's Mental Health is a national family-run organization linking more than 120 chapters and state organizations that focus on the issues of children and youth with emotional, behavioral, or mental health needs. In addition to providing local chapter information, the website has a wealth of resources about mental health and developmental issues, special education, respite, youth transition, and family advocacy.

CPSIA information can be obtained
at www.ICGtesting.com
Printed in the USA
LVOW04s0422311017

554384LV00001B/1/P